How t
Primary

CW01011163

For Aspiring Teachers,
Trainee Teachers and NQTs

The Future Teacher Foundation

Contents

Introduction

This book contains information for those thinking about becoming a primary school teacher and for those that have either begun their teacher training or are in the early stages of their teaching career.

It is intended to help those contemplating primary school teaching to: make a more informed decision about whether or not it is a suitable and feasible career choice for them, provide guidance on the realities and practicalities of applying for and undertaking Initial Teacher Education and Training (ITET) and offer an overview of the key aspects of the job and the structure of the education system.

Teachers who have already undertaken training will find this book full of useful tips and advice for enhancing their professional lives. This book is written predominantly for female teachers but the information is suitable for both genders. Men are encouraged to read the How to Become a Male Primary School Teacher book as it contains information specific to the challenges faced by men working in primary schools, this book is available on all Amazon Kindle enabled devices.

Many prospective teachers find it hard to know exactly what steps to take to start their journey. Many are confused and overwhelmed when researching teaching, and beginning their applications, due to the complexity of the process and lack of quality easy-to-understand information. Guidance is needed from the people who know the job best: currently serving teachers who are teaching in classrooms right now.

This book contains a complete, concise, modern summary of the job and offers guidance on every stage of application to begin ITET. You will learn how to gain experience in a school, assess all the financial implications before beginning teacher training, gain application, interview and personal statement advice as well as receiving information on every major teacher training route to becoming a primary school teacher. It also includes lots of tips and advice so you can begin your career in the best possible way; written collaboratively by currently serving primary school teachers keen to pass on their knowledge to you.

The information within this book should be used as a reference point for when you actually begin teaching or training. Learning to become a primary school teacher is such a vast and complicated process: gaining a quick understanding of the job is essential to ensure that you don't get left behind. This knowledge will not only give you a real head start when you begin your training, but also serve you well even if you have already begun teaching. In fact the book is designed so that you will find that when you re-read, even years into your teaching career, that different sections will resonate more with you and you will be enlightened with new learning that will enhance your professional life.

You may be starting out on a long held ambition to become a primary school teacher, be considering a career change later in life, or have completed a degree in an unrelated subject and found that job opportunities are scarce in the modern climate or that the realities of working in a specific field aren't what you'd previously thought. You may be considering your options for a degree, researching all potential future careers or just curious about what the job really involves. Whatever your situation, you have found the only resource of its kind that provides insights into modern primary school teaching created collaboratively to give you the maximum benefit of multiple perspectives, expertise and years of teaching experience.

We have endeavoured to communicate as succinctly as possible, without sacrificing quality, in order to pack as much information as we can into our book, whilst trying to still remain light enough to be an enjoyable read.

This advice will set your career of on the right path from the beginning. Knowing this at the start will give you a major advantage when you begin your teacher training whichever route you take whether it be School Direct,

PGCE or PDGE, Batchelor of Education, Teach First, The Welsh GTP, Troops to Teachers or working your way up the ladder as an unqualified teacher.

The Future Teacher Foundation

Qualities: Types of Person Suited to the Job

Is it for me?

"If you have knowledge, let others light their candles at it."

Margaret Fuller

This will be the question many of you are currently asking yourselves. Maybe you are questioning your suitability for the job, or just wondering if you can cut it as a primary school teacher and survive the notoriously hard training. For many the answer will be yes, for some, no.

Besides the relevant academic qualifications there are personal qualities you MUST have in order to become a primary school teacher.

1. You must like working with children and enjoy their company:

This may seem weird to you, but unfortunately there are adults working with children in this country who don't actually seem to like them! It may seem unbelievable to you reading this but people do go into this profession appearing to harbour negative feelings or a general disdain towards young people. Liking children and enjoying their company is the first major prerequisite of the job.

2. You must value knowledge and learning about the world:

Your day will be filled with imparting and sharing knowledge. You will need to gain a whole load of knowledge before you can even start teaching. If you are the sort of person who is ignorant to the world and doesn't respect knowledge then you have no place educating the next generation.

If you feel like you fulfil these two simple conditions then becoming a primary school teacher could indeed be for you. If not, then it is strongly recommended that you seriously consider your motives for this job, and whether it's really suitable for you.

Assuming you have decided that you easily meet this basic requirement and haven't stopped reading this book, we will continue to highlight other skills, characteristics and interests that suitable candidates may possess. None of these are pre-requisite but primary school teaching has elements of all of them and any combination will show you have potential:

- sporting interests
- creative interests
- artistic interests
- musical interests
- performance interests
- skills in maths and English
- wide general knowledge
- historical and geographical interests
- technological interests
- social work
- community minded
- helping people
- religious or spiritual interests
- organisational skills
- people and communication skills
- sense of humour
- enjoy working with other women
- enjoy having a laugh and being a bit silly

This list is not exhaustive but gives you an idea that if you possess a few of these characteristics or find these areas interesting then you are almost certainly a suitable personality for primary teaching and have something good to offer the next generation of young people.

What is it Really Like to Be a Primary School Teacher?

"Education is not the filling of a pail but the lighting of a fire."

W.B Yeats

What is it like to be a primary school teacher in the 21st century? Well, it's possibly very different to what you remember from school and definitely one of the few jobs in the United Kingdom that allows you to make a difference, and make the world a better place, every single working day. After becoming a primary school teacher you will be able to have a huge positive effect on young people's lives, so much so, that they may well indeed remember you into their adulthood and even for the rest of their time on Earth.

You will get to: inspire, educate, nurture and support children's minds, emotions and social skills. You will plan activities that get them excited about learning, making sure all abilities in the class achieve through the fun and informative delivery of your lessons. You will check their work and let them know what they have done well, and what they can do to improve next time. You will play a vital role, working in a close-knit team within a local community, helping and supporting the families in that area.

Sounds fantastic doesn't it? So why does there seem to be a perception amongst some in society that primary school teaching is a career to be looked down their nose at? The next section explores and contextualises just some of the associated misconceptions and stigmas around being a primary school teacher; exposing them for the ill-informed rubbish that they are.

You may have heard the demeaning phrase "those who can, do, and those who can't, teach," as if there is something inherently wrong, unsuccessful and degrading with trying to make the world a better place by sharing your knowledge and expertise and trying to help the next generation of young people towards a better future! This is besides the fact that, that doesn't make any sense regarding primary teaching - make this point if some imbecile says this to you.

You may also hear that teaching is not a job in the "real world," a comment whose rudeness is matched only by its ignorance. Working with children and families in a community setting, trying to help them by promoting knowledge and well-being is the REAL world you morons! Helping people and caring is way more real than spending your life in an office making money for some people who you're never going to meet and who don't care about you.

You see, there are many factors that contribute to the negative perception held by some about working as a primary school teacher. Sadly, this prevalent attitude is a product of the society we live in. As a capitalist democracy great importance and value is placed amongst the acquisition of wealth and status. The recent advent of the career woman and her increasingly acceptable status, high up the greasy pole, in previously male dominated work environments, has made it more aspirational and normal for degree educated women to join the corporate rat race.

Television programs like The Apprentice show us the new breed of corporate female who is willing and able to go head to head with the men for the spoils of the rat race. Some women (and men) buy into this mentality to the point where they would only consider working for a company or brand that they felt reflected their values or self-image, to the point where they would rather take a pay cut and work in the marketing department for Superdry as opposed to Poundland because it sounded less impressive and cool to other people. The point being made, is that when placed in this context, primary school teaching can be viewed as a poor relation by people who have this view of the world. The irony is that many of you reading this have experienced the corporate world and realised that it's not all that it's cracked up to be with its constant one-upmanship, competitiveness, pressures and falseness. Perhaps this is why you are seeking a more meaningful existence?

If you do face these kinds of prejudice when talking to people about becoming a primary school teacher, just remember that you will be joining a profession that puts other people first and allows you to nurture, care and laugh everyday with children and young people. If you think about it, it is clear who the more complete person is.

Another factor that combines with this is the perception that primary teaching is easy and the inferior option to secondary. This is simply not true. This book's intention is to give you facts and helpful opinions so that you can make a more informed decision if primary school teaching is feasible for you whilst providing key advice that will help you at any stage in your career. We must be honest with you. Primary teaching is no walk in the park. It can be a challenging job that has many tricky aspects. If you hold the misconception that primary school teachers start work at 9 and end at 3 (if only!) and that their day solely consists of sticking art work together, playing with Lego, reading stories and teaching the A-B-C then I'm afraid you are very much mistaken. Sorry to rain on your parade if you were hoping for a nice and easy namby-pamby job like that, but primary school teaching is a robust professional job with many facets and requirements, whilst it can be very enjoyable, fulfilling and rewarding, it is also a job nonetheless. In fact some would say more than just a job, and this is a good thing. You see, it is near impossible to be a primary school teacher without becoming emotionally attached to the job. Working with colleagues, children and families day in day out will get under your skin. But this is the great thing because you will be doing something that matters. Something that makes a difference. Something that's meaningful. Something that makes the world a better place, if only a little bit, every single day.

You see these are the real benefits. There simply aren't many jobs out there that allow you to share your innate nurturing and caring abilities, to see a difference every day by your actions and to genuinely help other people.

You see primary school teaching is a unique and wide ranging job. It is an incredibly emotionally and socially demanding job, which can be mentally demanding as well. The emotional and social aspects are something whose significance is not realised by many teachers. These are vital factors. So much so, that there is a whole chapter dedicated to understanding them in this book.

Other factors that are relevant to aspiring primary school teachers include that, due to working in a female dominated industry, it is less of a struggle to move forward in your careers and more accepted to see women in the higher places in the management hierarchies, if you are that way inclined. If not there are many other opportunities for career professional development. If you are more likely to start a family of your own or have young children, or just want to work less, there is a lot of opportunity for flexible working hours. You could work one or two days a week, do a job share, only work mornings or afternoons, do supply or even tuition work. This is all on top of a relatively generous maternity package especially when compared to private sector deals.

The National Curriculum

"The national curriculum is just one element in the education of every child. There is time and space in the school day and in each week, term and year to range beyond the national curriculum specifications."

National Curriculum in England DfE 2013

One advantage of primary school teaching over secondary is that you get to teach the full breadth of the national curriculum and more, ensuring a lot of variety to your working life. So if you're the sort of person with a wide variety of interests then this is a great way to engage in a lot of them. For example, you could be the type of person who has always done well in maths and English, but also enjoys sports or creative/artistic pursuits. Being a primary school teacher enables you to flex all these muscles. If, conversely, you are a physics graduate who has no interest in anything other than physics then maybe being a secondary school teacher would be more suitable.

Primary school teaching in England and Wales is currently in a state of transition to a new version of the national curriculum. The national curriculum is a document that outlines the statutory and non-statutory areas of learning that all state maintained (more on the different types of school in a following chapter) schools have to teach, this excludes academies, which are free to set their own broad and balanced curriculum. In Scotland the equivalent is called the Curriculum for Excellence and in Northern Ireland it is called the Northern Ireland Curriculum.

The new curriculum will have to be taught to all children (except those in academies) from September 2015. In September 2014 every year, except year 2 and year 6, will have to use the new curriculum. Here is a list of all the **old** national curriculum subjects taught in primary schools in England:

Maths

English including speaking and listening, writing and reading.

Science

History

Geography

Religious Education

Design and Technology (DT)

Art and design

Music

Physical education (P.E)

Modern foreign languages (MFL)

Social and emotional aspects of learning (SEAL)

Personal Social Health Education (PSHE)

Here is a list of all the **new** national curriculum subjects that will be taught in primary schools in England:

Core Subjects

English, including: spoken language, writing, reading, spelling, punctuation, vocabulary and grammar

Mathematics

Science

Foundation Subjects

Art and Design

Computing

Design and Technology

Geography

History

Languages

Music

Physical Education

Religious Education is also statutory and schools must make a provision for personal, social, health and economic education (PSHE).

The new curriculum is not vastly different on the surface, but the omission of statutory guidance on social and emotional aspects of learning (SEAL) is unfortunate, considering those skills underpin everything else and are genuine life skills that will help children become confident, kind, empathetic and happy adults. They are included in the overview section of the national curriculum so make sure you still make the effort to include such skills in your future teaching as these are aspects of learning that can really change children's lives.

As you can see you will be expected to deliver a broad curriculum. There is a lot to learn but you aren't expected to memorise it all. Plus as your experience grows you can easily tailor subjects to fit in with your interests, thus making the teaching more enthusiastic and usually the children more enthusiastic about their learning too.

There is a chance that some schools in your area may follow a slightly different curriculum due to their Academy status. This is a new type of school that the government has introduced that is free from local authority control and, as mentioned, can set their own curriculum. Don't worry though, their curriculum will almost certainly be similar in many ways to the list of previous subjects.

Different Ages and Stages of Education

"Learning is the only thing the mind never exhausts, never fears and never regrets."

Leonardo Da Vinci

This chapter will provide you with an overview of the organisation of children's education in the England and Wales. Scotland and Northern Ireland have a similar system but allocate different names to the age groups.

Foundation Stage One

This stage of education is non-compulsory and usually takes place in a pre-school or nursery environment and is for children aged between 3 and 4. The curriculum that's followed is called the Early Years Foundation Stage (EYFS) and is usually administered through well-planned play activities.

Foundation Stage Two

This stage of education caters for children aged between 4 and 5 and is often called the reception class when attached to an infant school or primary school. The EYFS curriculum is taught and this stage is also known by some as Key Stage Zero.

Key Stage One

Key stage one (KS1) consists of year one and year two. Year one is for children aged 5 to 6 and Year two is for children aged 6 to 7. The KS1 national curriculum is followed, although academies can set their own curriculum, there are statutory assessments that take place at the end of year two which academies also have to participate in and these are known as SATs.

Key Stage Two

Key stage 2 (KS2) consists of years three, four, five and six. Year three is for children aged between 7 and 8, year four is for children aged between 8 and 9, year five is for children aged between 9 and 10 and year six is for children aged between 10 and 11. Teaching follows the KS2 national curriculum, unless in an academy setting where they have the freedom to set their own curriculum, and there are statutory tests end of key stage tests at the end of year six known as SATs. Academies have to do these tests too and the results are made public for all schools.

Overview of the Main Types of Schools

"In teaching you cannot see the fruit of a day's work. It is invisible and remains so, maybe for twenty years."

Jacques Barzun

Schools are either state-funded or private. State-funded schools (sometimes referred to as community schools or maintained schools) are overseen by their local education authority unless they are academies which are independent from local authorities.

Primary Schools

Primary schools teach children typically from the ages of 4 to 11. Children enter in the foundation stage and leave in year six usually for secondary school education. All primary schools have foundation stages/reception classes attached to them and some have a nursery too. Primary schools are fully inclusive, meaning all children are welcome and all children should have their learning needs met. Primary schools teach the national curriculum and they have a certain amount of control over the way in which they choose to deliver the curriculum to the children.

Infant Schools

Infant schools are primary schools, but are distinguished by the age of the children that attend. Children will join aged 4 in the foundation stage and leave when they are 7 at the end of year two. This means that infant schools teach the Early Years Foundation Stage (EYFS) curriculum and the key stage one (KS1) national curriculum. This system is sometimes still called first schools in some parts of England and these schools may have children in there aged up to 9, but those are relatively uncommon.

Junior Schools

Junior schools are primary schools but are distinguished by the age of the pupils that they teach, they are the typical destination following infant school education. Children join at the start of year three aged 7 and stay until the end of year six aged 11. These four years are called key stage two (KS2).

Middle Schools

Middle schools are quite rare these days, middle schools who take mostly primary aged children are referred to as middle deemed-primaries. They accept children up to age 12 which means that they cross over from key stage two (KS2) to key stage three (KS3). Some middle schools are called middle deemed-secondary schools and these take children in at an older age, for example aged 9 (year five) to 13 (year nine).

If you are trained to teach primary you could find yourself working in one of these schools, they only exist in certain areas but would very interesting for you to visit, as a trainee or aspiring teacher, as they may have quite different approaches and atmospheres than primary schools, due to the older children that they accommodate as well.

Church of England Schools

Church of England (CofE) schools are fully inclusive schools which mean that they also accept children of other faiths and you do not need to be a Christian to work in one; they all promote diversity in their staffing. Maintained CofE schools follow the national curriculum and offer a broad and balanced school experience, Christianity and Christian values are likely to underpin a slightly larger proportion of the teaching and learning than in a school that has no affiliation to a specific religious faith. This will be to a lesser or greater extent depending on the school and a number of other variables. These variables include the head teacher, and whether or not the school is voluntary aided or voluntary controlled. Voluntary aided schools have closer links to the church and their governors have more influence whereas voluntary controlled schools work less closely with the church and more with the local authority, both types are also funded slightly differently.

Catholic Schools

Catholic schools are likely to mostly contain Catholic children, however they are fully inclusive, admitting children from all faiths and backgrounds. You do not need to be a Catholic to work in one, although a sensitivity and respect of their values and ethos would be advised if hoping to work or train in one. Catholic schools that aren't academies have to teach the national curriculum and they offer a broad and balanced school experience but there will be a strong influence from Catholic values underpinning more of the learning than in a school unaffiliated to a church or religion. This will be the case in varying degrees as all school are slightly different.

Academies

Academies are a relatively new type of school and an interesting aspect of modern day primary school teaching. Academies are publicly funded schools that do not need to follow the national curriculum, they can set pay and conditions for staff and are allowed to set their own term times. Academies get their funding from the government but are free from local authority control allowing them greater flexibility in how they spend their budgets. Some academies have sponsors such as universities, businesses, other schools, faith or voluntary groups.

Private or Independent Schools

These schools are funded by charging fees to attend, they do not take money from the government and they do not have to follow the national curriculum. These schools are inspected, half of which by Ofsted and rest by either the Independent Schools Inspectorate, The Bridge Schools Inspectorate or the School inspection service. Staff can be paid slightly more than in state schools and receive longer holidays although there may be a greater expectation to run more after school activities.

Free Schools

Free schools are a new type of school that are funded by the government but aren't run by the local authority. They are not allowed to use an academic selection process like grammar schools making them more inclusive. Free schools do not need to follow the national curriculum, can set pay and conditions for staff and are allowed to set their own term times. Free schools are run on a not for profit basis and can be set up by institutions or groups such as universities, charities, faith groups or businesses.

How to Become a Primary School Teacher: Routes into Teaching

> *"The aim of education should be to teach us rather how to think, than what to think — rather to improve our minds, so as to enable us to think for ourselves, than to load the memory with thoughts of other men."*
>
> Bill Beattie

This chapter provides a summary of all the most conventional training options available. The range of teacher training options can be hard to understand, the aim of this chapter is to simplify the process of getting to grips with understanding it all. This information is available in a similar form from our website. We have decided to include the information because some of you may have purchased this book without visiting the website, it is also convenient to have it for everyone in case you need the information and you do not have access to the internet. These are the practicalities, being a primary school teacher is so much more fulfilling than this.

What do I Need to Get to Become a Primary School Teacher?

To teach in most primary age schools you need to gain Qualified Teacher Status (QTS) or a Teaching Qualification (TQ) if based in Scotland. This is got through Initial Teacher Education and Training (ITET) which comes in a variety of forms. Check your current status against these options.

I Have No Degree Yet

You can get a degree which comes with QTS or do a degree in something else and go for a postgraduate teacher training course as well. A degree with QTS is usually a Bachelor of Education (BEd) but could be a Bachelor of Science/Arts degree. You will typically need GCSE grades A-C in English, maths and Science and at least two A-levels (see the following chapter's route fact files for more information). You may be able to access with different qualifications, especially if you are a mature student, check with your desired university or through the UCAS teacher training website which is the new centre for all teacher training routes, excluding Teach First.

I Have a Degree in Something Else

You will need to go down the postgraduate route. If your degree is completely unrelated to National Curriculum core-subjects (maths, English) you may need to undertake a further training course to ensure your knowledge is up to scratch, but this is unlikely. There are a few options for you. You could do a Postgraduate Certificate in Education (PGCE), which can be full-time or part time and are typically one year with placements in schools. This is called a Professional Graduate Diploma in Education (PGDE) in Scotland.

Another option is to take part in the government's new School Direct Training program which trains high quality graduates in schools in England and Scotland (Welsh candidates would need to apply for the Welsh GTP). There are two options the first pays you a salary to train and the second requires you to pay the tuition fees, there are loans and grants available. There is another option if you have a degree and also lots of experience working and teaching in a school as an unqualified teacher or higher level teaching assistant; this is called the Assessment Only route.

Other Requirements

You will also need to pass two skills tests in literacy and numeracy before you begin your training and of course, you will need a disclosure from the Disclosure and Barring Service (DBS) proving that you haven't been barred from working with young people or vulnerable adults.

In Summary

So basically you either need an education specific degree with QTS, or a degree in something else that doesn't come with QTS which is then enhanced with another, usually year long, postgraduate training course afterwards. This is either on the job training, or doing college/university based learning with placements in schools. You also need at least a C grade GCSE, or equivalent in English, maths and science. If you don't have those GCSE's you can re-take them through many establishments and they are called GCSE equivalence tests.

If you understand this so far, then you are doing very well! You will surely make an excellent teacher. The following chapter examines each training route in more detail. Each teacher training route has its own fact file containing application information and other key facts.

Routes into Teaching Fact Files and How to Apply

"The secret of success is constancy of purpose."

Benjamin Disraeli

Route: School Direct Training Program (Salaried).

Where is it based: In a high quality primary school.

Who is it for: Career changers - high quality graduates.

What are the entry requirements: A UK undergraduate degree or equivalent, rated first class or 2:1, three years' experience in a job and GCSE grades (or equivalent) at C or above in maths English and science.

How long is the course: One year resulting in QTS.

How do you learn to teach: On the job training working in a real school combined with workshops, lectures and training from an outside accredited School Centred Initial Teacher Training (SCITT) provider.

Where is this available: In England and Scotland at schools that have registered with School Direct. Once you have applied and are successful you will be placed with a school in your area.

How do you apply: Through the UCAS teacher training website.

Main advantages: Getting paid to train and learning on the job from real teachers in a real school whilst also gaining knowledge from workshops, lectures and tutorials.

Other information: This route is highly competitive. Experience in a school or working with children will help to give you the edge. You will also need to have passed the literacy and numeracy professional skills tests before you begin your training.

Route: School Direct Training Program (Fee Paying).

Where is it based: In a high quality primary school.

Who is it for: High quality graduates.

What are the entry requirements: A UK undergraduate degree or equivalent and GCSE grades (or equivalent) at C or above in maths English and science.

How long is the course: One year resulting in QTS.

How do you learn to teach: On the job training working in a real school combined with workshops, lectures and training from an outside accredited School Centred Initial Teacher Training (SCITT) provider.

Where is this available: In England and Scotland at schools that have registered with School Direct. Once you have applied and are successful you will be placed with a school in your area.

How do you apply: Through the UCAS teacher training website.

Main advantages: Learning on the job from real teachers in a real school whilst also gaining knowledge from workshops, lectures and tutorials.

Other information: Whilst you will have to pay fees for the training, grants and bursaries are available to help cover the costs and to help with your living expenses, if you met the criteria. This route is highly competitive. Experience in a school or working with children will help to give you the edge. You will also need to have passed the literacy and numeracy professional skills tests before you begin your training.

Route: Postgraduate Certificate in Education (PGCE or PDGE in Scotland).

Where is it based: University or college based training.

Who is it for: High quality graduates.

What are the entry requirements: A UK undergraduate degree or equivalent and GCSE grades (or equivalent) at C or above in maths English and science.

How long is the course: One year full-time, two years part-time resulting in QTS and a PGCE or PDGE.

How do you learn to teach: College or university based learning with twenty four weeks in a real school.

Where is this available: All across the U.K at universities and colleges.

How do you apply: Through the UCAS teacher training website.

Main advantages: A refined blend of lectures and twenty four weeks of real life experience in two schools, plus the chance to have a university or college experience again. You will also have the opportunity to make new friends with the other trainees; the shared experience and support will help you through the training.

Other information: Whilst you will have to pay fees for the training, grants and bursaries are available to help cover the costs if you met the criteria. This route is highly competitive. Experience in a school or working with children will help to give you the edge. You will also need to have passed the literacy and numeracy professional skills tests before you begin your training.

Route: Degree with Qualified Teacher Status (QTS).

Where is it based: University or college based training.

Who is it for: Candidates without a degree and the entry requirements.

What are the entry requirements: It varies from different providers but generally two A-levels or a BTEC National Diploma (both of these may be subject specific so check with your desired establishment). You may also be able to enter with an Access to Higher Education Diploma and some CACHE diplomas. You typically, must also have C grades or equivalent in maths, English and science.

How long is the course: Three to four years full-time or four to six years part-time.

How do you learn to teach: Comprehensive university lecture based training with school placements.

Where is this available: All across the U.K at universities and colleges.

How do you apply: Through the UCAS teacher training website. Apply early as places are limited.

Main advantages: No additional PGCE or School Direct postgraduate course is required and the length of the course gives you an in depth understanding of the complex world of primary school teaching.

Other information: Whilst you will have to pay fees for the training, grants and bursaries are available to help cover the costs if you met the criteria and student loans are also available. Degrees are usually Batchelor of Education (BEd) but there are some Batchelor of Arts (BA) or Batchelor of Science (BSc) degrees that also award QTS including Early Years Education which focuses on teaching the age range of 3-7.

Route: Teach First.

Where is it based: University then school based.

Who is it for: Candidates with leadership potential.

What are the entry requirements: A 2:1 degree or higher, a C grade or above in maths, English and science and a demonstration of your potential that shows your values match those of the charity.

How long is the course: Two years in total.

How do you learn to teach: Six weeks intensive training then two years working in a school in a challenging school usually in a low-income area resulting in a PGCE

Where is this available: Nine regions across England Wales.

How do you apply: Through the Teach First website.

Main advantages: A strong likelihood that you will be given a job at the end. You are also more likely to get to leadership or management positions more quickly.

Other information: Just like the School Direct salaried scheme you will be paid a minimum rate that is equivalent to an unqualified teacher salary, this is around £15,000 a year.

Route: Graduate Teacher Training in Wales (GTP).

Where is it based: School based.

Who is it for: Welsh graduates.

What are the entry requirements: A high quality degree and at least a C grade in GCSE maths, English and science.

How long is the course: One year.

How do you learn to teach: By working in a school and attending workshops and training by local providers.

Where is this available: Via one of the three centres of Teacher Education and Training either North and Mid Wales, South East Wales and South West Wales.

How do you apply: Contact the nearest centre for Teacher Education and Training.

Main advantages: Learning on the job from real teachers in the classroom and getting paid a salary to do so.

Other information: You will be paid a salary during this training equating to approximately £15,000 a year.

Route: Troops to Teachers.

Where is it based: School based with one day at university.

Who is it for: Outstanding service leavers without a degree either two years before or after leaving.

What are the entry requirements: Sufficient evidence of specialist subject knowledge and academic achievement. It is best to contact the scheme directly if you are unsure whether or not you fulfil these conditions.

How long is the course: Two years.

How do you learn to teach: Four days a week in a school and one day a week in a university.

Where is this available: Universities across England including Brighton, Bath Spa, Canterbury, Huddersfield, Reading, Southampton and Staffordshire.

How do you apply: Through the Troops to Teachers website.

Main advantages: A great paid route for former servicemen that provides excellent benefits compared to other routes into teaching.

Other information: You could be paid up to 80% of an unqualified teacher's salary. This could equate to roughly £12,000 a year.

Route: Assessment only (AO), evidence based route to QTS.

Where is it based: School based.

Who is it for: Candidates with a U.K degree or equivalent possessing significant experience in teaching. An example of this would be a higher level teaching assistant (HLTA).

What are the entry requirements: Lots of experience and evidence that shows you have the ability to meet the standards for QTS. You also need a school that will sponsor you to complete, and the standard C grade or equivalent qualification in English, maths and science. You will need to have passed the skills tests and have experienced teaching in at least two schools.

How long is the course: This isn't a course, the idea is that you need no further training to meet the standards for QTS, but you will be subject to a thorough and rigorous examination and this process of assessment shouldn't last longer than three months.

How do you learn to teach: You would already possess an extensive knowledge.

Where is this available: Universities and colleges across England provide the assessment, and are called AO providers but the process will a largely take place in the host school.

How do you apply: Contact your local AO provider via the government's Get into Teaching website.

Main advantages: A great route if you feel you meet the criteria and require no further training.

Other information: Fees average out at around £2300. This route is usually self-funded but your school may be able to help.

Route: Becoming a Primary School Teacher without a Degree.

If you are in the situation of wanting to become a primary school teacher and you do not have a degree then, excluding the assessment only (AO) route, you basically need to get a degree. You could teach in an academy or possibly in a private school as an unqualified teacher but to gain QTS and be able to teach in the vast majority of schools you need to possess a degree.

There are so many different circumstances and variables in situation for people without degrees that it is impossible to account for them all. But there are lots of routes to a degree that you could take. Many of these involve a lot of effort over a long period of time but if you are committed and determined to change your life and follow your dream then time is no obstacle to overcome. You just need to make sure you get all the qualifications you need before each stage. For example, if you check the requirements of your local university or college you may find that they will accept candidates onto QTS degree courses with certain National Diploma qualifications, you would then need to find out where you could get that National Diploma from and check the entry requirements to that. Whichever route you take it would certainly be wise, if you think you need to, to begin improving your skills in numeracy and literacy to ensure you can meet the standards required to pass the skills tests.

 If you are already a teaching assistant or thinking of becoming one, then maybe becoming a Higher Level Teaching Assistant (HLTA) could be an option as having done this for a few years and gained varied experience, you may well eligible to apply for the Assessment Only (AO) route to QTS if you undertook an open university degree at the same time.

The Literacy and Numeracy Skills Tests

These tests are to ensure that all teachers who are awarded QTS have met a baseline standard for skills in numeracy and literacy. The tests are not easy and do require preparation. Re-takes are available, but not indefinitely, so passing first time is highly preferable. If you do not pass these tests, then you cannot be awarded QTS. It is now required that these tests must be passed before any Initial Teacher Training and Education course or degree begins. This is a positive step as in the past, teacher trainees were finding that they were in the position where they had invested years of time and money into completing their training only to keep failing the skills tests. At least this way any candidates who can't reach the required level won't have wasted too much time and money.

Qualified Teacher Status (QTS) and Teachers' Standards

"Most teachers have little control over school policy or curriculum or choice of texts or special placement of students, but most have a great deal of autonomy inside the classroom. To a degree shared by only a few other occupations, such as police work, public education rests precariously on the skill and virtue of the people at the bottom of the institutional pyramid."

Tracy Kidder

QTS enables you to teach in state-maintained schools in England and Wales and in special schools. Academies do not require teachers to have QTS and neither do private schools. QTS is awarded once you have finished your teacher training and met the professional standards, you also need to have passed the skills tests in numeracy and literacy, but new (anyone didn't start their training before the 1st of July 2013) applicants will have needed to pass these to be accepted onto Initial Teacher Training anyway. Most teachers who have qualified as a teacher outside of England and Wales can have their credentials checked to see if they are suitable to be awarded QTS for England and Wales if they wish to teach in these countries. This is done by the National College for Teaching and Leadership (NCTL).

QTS Professional Standards

You will be assessed against these standards to see if you can be recommended for QTS and evidence will need to be provided to show you meet each one. Don't worry if at first they seem intimidating and confusing, as you progress through your teacher training your understanding of each aspect will develop. As you gain evidence against each standard, you will also see how many of the activities and events you document can be cross-referenced against each other, resulting in multiple standards being evidenced at once. The following information regarding Teachers' Standards has been used with permission and contains information from the original document that is entitled Teachers' Standards - Reference: DFE-00066-2011 - V5.0 05.06.13 and can be downloaded from www.education.gov.uk

PART ONE: TEACHING

A teacher must:

1. Set high expectations which inspire, motivate and challenge pupils

- establish a safe and stimulating environment for pupils, rooted in mutual respect
- set goals that stretch and challenge pupils of all backgrounds, abilities and dispositions
- demonstrate consistently the positive attitudes, values and behaviour which are expected of pupils.

2. Promote good progress and outcomes by pupils

- be accountable for pupils' attainment, progress and outcomes
- be aware of pupils' capabilities and their prior knowledge, and plan teaching to build on these
- guide pupils to reflect on the progress they have made and their emerging needs
- demonstrate knowledge and understanding of how pupils learn and how this impacts on teaching
- encourage pupils to take a responsible and conscientious attitude to their own work and study.

3. Demonstrate good subject and curriculum knowledge

- have a secure knowledge of the relevant subject(s) and curriculum areas, foster and

maintain pupils' interest in the   subject, and
address misunderstandings
- demonstrate a critical understanding of
developments in the subject and curriculum
areas, and promote the value of scholarship
- demonstrate an understanding of and take
responsibility for promoting high standards of
.literacy, articulacy and the correct use of
standard English, whatever the teacher's
specialist subject
- if teaching early reading, demonstrate a clear
understanding of systematic synthetic phonics
- if teaching early mathematics, demonstrate a
clear understanding of appropriate teaching
strategies.

4. Plan and teach well structured lessons

- impart knowledge and develop understanding
through effective use of lesson time
- promote a love of learning and children's
intellectual curiosity
- set homework and plan other out-of-class
activities to consolidate and extend the
knowledge and understanding pupils have
acquired
- reflect systematically on the effectiveness of
lessons and approaches to teaching
- contribute to the design and provision of an
engaging curriculum within the relevant subject
area(s).

5. Adapt teaching to respond to the strengths and needs of all pupils

- know when and how to differentiate appropriately, using approaches which enable pupils to be taught effectively
- have a secure understanding of how a range of factors can inhibit pupils' ability to learn, and how best to overcome these
- demonstrate an awareness of the physical, social and intellectual development of children, and know how to adapt teaching to support pupils' education at different stages of development
- have a clear understanding of the needs of all pupils, including those with special educational needs; those of high ability; those with English as an additional language; those with disabilities; and be able to use and evaluate distinctive teaching approaches to engage and support them.

6. Make accurate and productive use of assessment

- know and understand how to assess the relevant subject and curriculum areas, including statutory assessment requirements
- make use of formative and summative assessment to secure pupils' progress
- use relevant data to monitor progress, set targets, and plan subsequent lessons

46

- give pupils regular feedback, both orally and through accurate marking, and encourage pupils to respond to the feedback.

7. Manage behaviour effectively to ensure a good and safe learning environment

- have clear rules and routines for behaviour in classrooms, and take responsibility for promoting good and courteous behaviour both in classrooms and around the school, in accordance with the school's behaviour policy
- have high expectations of behaviour, and establish a framework for discipline with a range of strategies, using praise, sanctions and rewards consistently and fairly
- manage classes effectively, using approaches which are appropriate to pupils' needs in order to involve and motivate them
- maintain good relationships with pupils, exercise appropriate authority, and act decisively when necessary.

8. Fulfil wider professional responsibilities

- make a positive contribution to the wider life and ethos of the school
- develop effective professional relationships with colleagues, knowing how and when to draw on advice and specialist support
- deploy support staff effectively

- take responsibility for improving teaching through appropriate professional development, responding to advice and feedback from colleagues
- communicate effectively with parents with regard to pupils' achievements and well-being.

PART TWO: PERSONAL AND PROFESSIONAL CONDUCT

A teacher is expected to demonstrate consistently high standards of personal and professional conduct. The following statements define the behaviour and attitudes which set the required standard for conduct throughout a teacher's career.

• Teachers uphold public trust in the profession and maintain high standards of ethics and behaviour, within and outside school, by:

- treating pupils with dignity, building relationships rooted in mutual respect, and at all times observing proper boundaries appropriate to a teacher's professional position

- having regard for the need to safeguard pupils' well-being, in accordance with statutory provisions

- showing tolerance of and respect for the rights of others

- not undermining fundamental British values, including democracy, the rule of law, individual liberty and mutual respect, and tolerance of those with different faiths and beliefs

- ensuring that personal beliefs are not expressed in ways which exploit pupils' vulnerability or might lead them to break the law.

• Teachers must have proper and professional regard for the ethos, policies and practices of the school in which they teach, and maintain high standards in their own attendance and punctuality.

• Teachers must have an understanding of, and always act within, the statutory frameworks which set out their professional duties and responsibilities.

Newly Qualified Teacher (NQT) Induction

This three-term period begins once you have gained QTS. This is usually done in one school and called an NQT year, but as the "three-term" period suggests it can be completed in a number of schools and not necessarily in one year, it can also be completed part-time. During the induction you will receive personalised guidance and support and be assessed against the Teachers' Standards at the end of each term to ensure you are on-track to succeed and to highlight areas of development. During this period you will be entitled to have 10% of your working week allocated for developing your teaching skills outside of the classroom and another 10% of your time for planning, preparation and assessment (PPA). This means, assuming you are working full-time, that you should only be teaching in front of your class for four days a week.

Assuming successful completion of all the requirements involved in meeting the Teachers Standards at a NQT level, your training will culminate in receiving notice from the National College for Teaching and Leadership that you have successfully completed your NQT induction and you are now officially a teacher! Congratulations, you've made it!

Financial Considerations in Becoming a Primary School Teacher

"Dreams do come true, if we only wish hard enough, you can have anything in life if you will sacrifice everything else for it."

James M. Barrie

Depending on your current circumstances in life, the financial realities of training to become a primary school teacher may or may not be playing on your mind. For many it will be one of the key questions they are asking themselves.

If you are an older prospective primary school teacher then you may well have children of your own, a mortgage and bills to pay whilst possibly taking the financial hit of reducing your income while you train. You have probably been asking yourself if the figures add up and if you actually can afford it. This chapter will provide you with the facts regarding the financial considerations involved in each route to becoming a primary school teacher and some food for thought as you work through the viability of making the leap to beginning teacher training. It is a massive decision with many aspects and does need to be researched, planned and discussed with all parties concerned thoroughly. If you are younger or have less financial responsibilities as you begin your journey, then this chapter still holds valuable insights for you concerning the time teacher training will take up and your potential future salaries. You will maybe also learn to appreciate how relatively simple your journey may be.

For all routes into teaching there are a variety of options available to help with the costs involved. Funding has recently been reorganised to assist and encourage the government's most desirable postgraduate candidates into teaching. Some routes will pay your fees and pay you a salary to train and others will require you to pay the fees yourself. In all cases where fees are payable by you, there are bursaries (which do not need to be paid back) available for candidates who meet the criteria of having a 2:1 or above in their degree and/or a desirable subject specialism like maths (maths specialist with a 2:2 may be eligible also). Other options for financing include student loans which are designed to be repayable in instalments, but only after you start earning £21,000 and means tested (income and living circumstances related) grants and loans that are available from the government's student finance website. Exact specifications will follow as we explore each route.

The salaried School Direct training route pays approximately £15,000 for the year. This option actually pays you a salary to complete the training, places are limited and there are entrance criteria but that doesn't mean it's impossible to get on, the places have to be filled by someone.

The other, fee paying, School Direct scheme will require you to pay tuition fees which should be around £6000, however some establishments have been charging up to £9000. There are Training bursaries available to candidates with certain subject specialisms like maths, or if you have 2:1 degree or higher. There are also loans, grants and maintenance loans available to help with all the costs.

Undertaking a PGCE will normally cost £9000 for UK/EU students (sometimes more for overseas candidates) for the year's tuition fees, but like the School Direct fee paying option, there are training bursaries available. There is also the more common route of getting a student loan from the student finance government website. There may well be other means tested maintenance grants that you could be eligible for. You should check with your training provider.

Beginning a Batchelor of Education (BEd) degree which results in qualified teacher status (QTS) will last three or four years and will have tuition fees normally very close to £9000 a year. There are student loans, bursaries and maintenance grants available to help with the funding involved in obtaining a degree. You should check the specifics and eligibility with your chosen university or college.

All of these teacher training routes do not account for the other costs you may incur during the training period which could include: living expenses, travel, textbooks, GCSE retakes, stationary, computing costs and administrative consumables like printer cartridges or memory sticks.

Whichever option is the one for you, once your training is complete and you have received QTS you will begin your newly qualified teacher (NQT) induction period. Assuming you have got yourself a full time teaching job, with your very own class, you will be paid a minimum of £21,804 a year or £27,270 if you work in inner London.

GCSE Retakes or Equivalence Tests

GCSE retakes or equivalence tests are available in a variety of locations around the country. Some institutions offer 10-12 week courses that will tutor you to the test, and these cost around £250. The actual test itself without tuition will cost around £100 and most places offer 2 free resits if you don't make the grade. A good way to approach these is to try to learn the information yourself. By doing this you will give your teaching career a massive boost as you can re-learn, how to learn. You will find out how you learn the best and these self-motivating initiative skills will serve you very well when you have a mountain of new learning to scale, when you do start to train to be a primary school teacher. There are many books and on-line resources to help with the subject knowledge required to pass the tests; a great place to start is the BBC GCSE Bitesize website.

Financial planning

The best option, if you are still unsure of the feasibility, would be to create a long term financial plan. Firstly you need to work out all of your current outgoings and fixed costs. Get a recent bank statement or two and find out exactly where your money is going; this will give you your current cost of living. It is a good idea to work this out including and excluding your food bill and obtaining a figure that is just your bills and essentials for living. Once this is done you could see if there are any extraneous costs that you are regularly spending money on, that you might be able to cut back on if needs be. For example, if you added up the costs of all the nights out, coffee shop coffees and meals out that you eat in restaurants and takeaways, you may be surprised how much it adds up too. This will clarify your exact financial position as it is and where all your money goes. If the idea of cutting back on your life sends a shiver down your spine, be strong; remember that it's short term pain for long term gain.

The next step would be to map out the future time it would take for you to complete your training from start to finish. An example would be if you were on the salaried School Direct scheme then you would know that you would be receiving £15,000 a year, which after tax leaves approximately £1000 a month. You will be able to match up your income with your expenditure and see how they compare. Maybe you will get a shock or maybe you will begin to see that actually this will be very achievable for you will a small amount of discipline and sacrifice of those daily coffee shop coffees! You may even find that you would have a few months beforehand that would allow you to put aside some money for the training year or even begin to see how you could do a job in the evenings or at weekends to supplement your income like tuition; which can earn around £15-30 an hour. The trick is to start asking yourself empowering problem solving questions like "how can I afford this?" or "what can I do to make this work?" Once you know where you stand, the picture will become a lot clearer of your future, and the task far less daunting.

If you are feeling overwhelmed by the potential financial strain of training to become a primary school teacher or the leap from a secure wage to an uncertain one is weighing heavily on your mind, you must remember that nothing will change by staying the same and to follow your dreams you sometimes need to endure short term pain for long term gain.

How to get Experience in a School

"Nothing ever becomes real 'til it is experienced."

John Keats

Why is Experience Important?

Primary schools have changed quite a lot since when you were there. Even if you left relatively recently, there have been many changes in the last few years - with many more currently occurring. To get an understanding of modern primary school teaching and the working life of a modern primary school teacher, it is essential that you take a fresh look from an adult's perspective, speak to and observe real teachers and get a feel for the modern day realities of the job by offering to help out in a primary school.

Having some experience in a school is vital if you are serious about becoming a primary school teacher. This is especially relevant if you are a career changer, later on in life. Competition for places on the School Direct scheme and PGCE's are limited and very competitive in most areas of the country and time spent in a school will give your chances of successfully getting on the training a major boost. If you are planning to start a degree then spending a day or a week in a primary school will serve to give you valuable experience ahead of your course, and even benefit you in your course application or entrance interview, if you are required to have one.

If you are still just thinking about becoming a primary school teacher it would certainly be wise to spend some time in an actual school just to ensure that you don't have any huge misconceptions about the job and to check that it is actually a suitable environment for you to work in. It's better to find out if it isn't early on, rather than a year down the line and a few thousand pounds in debt. Another possible benefit is that you may well indeed impress the management at the school who in turn either offer you more opportunities there or keep you in mind for future work. They may well even see real potential in you and be willing to sponsor you as a teacher trainee in their school.

Typical Routes to Gaining Experience

The route that will be most suitable for you to take will be dictated by your age, circumstances or what you are willing to give up that will enable you to get into a primary school. The most common approach, and one that is suitable for all, is the simple method of approaching a local school and simply asking if it is at all possible for you to come in and help them for free, by listening to readers or helping out in class as a voluntary teaching assistant.

If you are still in education then you may have the opportunity to spend time in a school as part of a work experience week or job placement scheme. This chance should be snapped up, so speak to your careers advisor, college or university and find whoever is responsible for organising the placements as soon as you can. If this time has passed or for whatever reason this option is not possible, then you should speak to as many of your teachers or lecturers as you can about getting some time in a primary school. Many of these will have connections to primary or junior schools in the area and there may well be someone who knows someone, who can help you out with that vital contact.

If you are working in the private sector and considering a career change then maybe your workplace, as part of their corporate responsibility scheme, has the option for you to spend some of your working week helping out in a primary school?

Disclosure and Barring Service (DBS) Checks

As long as you do not have regular and unsupervised contact with children you will not be required to have Disclosure and Barring Service (DBS) clearance, previously called the CRB. This formal police records check shows whether or not you have any criminal convictions in your past and particularly highlights anything that prevents you from working with children or young people. As long as you are supervised, which you will be, then this is currently not required for entering a school and volunteering in this way. It is best to discuss this with the school to make sure. Depending on the exact circumstances, they may prefer, or be required, to get one for you which would likely be a volunteer certificate which is free of charge.

If you do have incidents from your past on your police record and you are concerned as to whether or not they may affect you in becoming a primary school teacher, then you will need to seek specific advice from the DBS. As a rule of thumb, there are certain serious convictions that would rule you out immediately and other more minor offences that should be overlooked. But it does depend on the person who is making that decision, this may be a teacher training provider, a head teacher or even a parent governor in an interview situation. You may come up against someone who has a particular issue with whatever misdemeanour you have got caught doing, and an unwillingness to hear how you have learnt from and overcome this mistake. It is a shame that a mistake made in your distant past, that has no negative consequence on who you are now or your ability to become an outstanding teacher, could come back to hinder you in becoming a primary school teacher, but this is the reality of the situation.

Crucial Factors and Key Questions Regarding Experience

When making decisions about how to get experience in a school there are some key questions you need to ask yourself and crucial factors to be aware of.

Could you work as a teaching assistant for a year?

This question has been asked first for a reason. Becoming a teaching assistant is the best experience you can get for becoming a primary school teacher. You would: get the space and time to understand teaching and school life without the pressure of actually having to teach lessons, get paid for gaining significant experience in working with children and helping their learning, get to analyse teaching and learning and build up your own understanding, develop a deep understanding that would separate you from the competition in interview and application scenarios, speak to many teachers and other school staff, make new contacts and friends and potentially even find a school that would sponsor your training but most importantly...You would know what it's like to be a teaching assistant. This knowledge alone will enhance your professional life immeasurably when you finally begin teaching; a successful and productive working relationship with your teaching assistants is absolutely vital for outstanding teaching and a positive working life.

Finding a job as a teaching assistant may not be easy and it might be an idea to work for free in a school to show your aptitude. Interviews are usually competitive as it is a very desirable job for mums of school age children, but if you have the chance to do this then whatever your current situation it is highly recommended. If this is not feasible for whatever reason do not fear, there are many other options available that will give you the experience you require.

Can you work for free?

If you are unwilling or unable to offer any of your time for free then you will probably be facing quite a challenge to get experience in a primary school. Being able to give up your time for no money enables you to be a more appealing proposition to a school and shows that you are serious about teaching. If you can offer your time for free then you stand a better chance of gaining the vital experience. Think of it as an investment in your future.

How much time do you have to spare?

If you have plenty of spare time, or could free up a day or two a week or even every morning, for primary school experience then that is fantastic, your flexibility will increase your options. If you are in full time employment and giving away so much time is simply not an option, then taking a week off work as holiday or unpaid leave could be your best option. You could use that time to spend an entire week in a primary school or even spread over a few different schools in your local area.

Could you work a part-time job and volunteer in a school?

Would it be possible for you to work a part-time job, say maybe at weekends or in the evenings, which would enable you to have enough money to live for a time so that you had free time in the week for volunteering? This is usually a more suitable option for younger primary school teaching candidates with less financial responsibilities than later-in-life career changers. However, it is always an option for those more mature potential primary school teachers, as long as the figures add up (more on this in a following chapter) or if they have a friend, relative or partner that can support them through the reduction in income for a short period.

Do you have any possible contacts that could help you?

You need to be creative when answering this question. We don't all have a head teacher for a mum! So ask yourself is there anyone you know that could give you a "foot in the door" at a friendly primary school? If there is then you need to ask/bribe this person to help you! This could even be as tenuous a link as just knowing a parent who has a child in a school who is willing to accompany you to the front office and vouch for you and introduce you to the head teacher, deputy head or the office staff, where you can politely inquire as to any volunteering opportunities (more on what to say later). Or you could even approach your old school, if you are in your local area, seeing an old face or having the chance to help a former pupil interested in becoming a teacher would delight most schools.

If you do have any contacts then that is a major advantage and you should leverage them to get you into a school, if you do not, then do not fear...

No contacts….No worries!

If you are in the position that you do not have any links to a school or know anyone that can put you in touch with the right person then that is unfortunate, but all is not lost, all you need to do is approach a school in the right way.

How to Approach a School

A good blend of politeness, persistence and enthusiasm mixed with an understanding and appreciation of the school will set you on the right path when approaching a primary school for experience.

You need to communicate that you are seriously considering becoming a primary school teacher and that you would love to have the opportunity to help out the children and staff by volunteering your time for free to help out round the school in any way possible. One potential way in would be to offer to work with small groups, hear readers or to help with an after school club.

As previously mentioned, if you have a contact who can introduce you, that is highly preferable to "going in cold" but if you don't then you have one of three options: email, phone or visit.

You could email a school to explain your circumstances and how you would love to volunteer in their school whilst politely enquiring about any opportunities to help them out that they may be able to offer you. The best way would be to approach the school directly and to speak to whoever is in the school office. These days you may need to speak through an intercom system before you actually meet a human face-to-face, but a sunny disposition and good manners should see you through to someone who can actually offer what you need.

Phoning also has advantages but be aware that people are busy at work and usually do not have too long to chat on the phone and also as a warning, some schools let the children answer the phone at certain times of the days so watch out for that! A phone call at best may get you a short interview or just an invitation to visit the school, or at worst a negative response from a someone who denies you any opportunity to help, if that's the case then do not despair, simply try another school or better yet go back and visit that school's office in person, try a slightly different approach and you never know, the result could be different. At least you know you will have tried everything to get into that particular school.

Once you are in the school you have a golden opportunity to learn and gain that valuable experience that will serve you so well, but you must behave in the correct manner and make the most of the opportunity you have created for yourself.

How to Conduct Yourself and Maximise the Opportunity

Assuming that you have managed to get yourself some experience helping out in a local school for a week, it is very important that you are aware of needs of the adults and the children in school. You would be there for your own benefit - but you need to be mostly benefitting the other adults and of course the children and their learning. By this we mean pick and choose your time wisely to ask the teachers questions, and make sure that when you are working with children you are trying to help them learn and not just having a laugh with them. Good things could come from this for you and people talk to each other, gaining a good reputation even over a few days could lead to more work, a teaching assistant role or, the holy grail of a sponsored teacher training placement at the school.

Before entering the school you need to be very clear in your mind what your key questions are and what you are hoping to get out of the experience. This information will be personal to you and depend on your knowledge about teaching and your certainty about how committed you are in following through with this as a profession. This will help you to know what you need to get out of the experience and enable you to assess how much you are learning as you go through the week. Primary school teaching is a massive subject and a huge job, so don't be alarmed if you come away with more questions than when you started!

Finding a nice teacher that will happily spend some time with you discussing teaching shouldn't be too hard. If you politely inquire by saying something along the lines of "I know you are really busy but is there any chance I could have five minutes to talk to you about your job?" then you should be on to a winner. People love to talk about themselves and teachers love to talk about teaching, it is such an all-encompassing job that you have to talk about it a lot just to help your brain process it all. Asking for five minutes, will appear as if you're not asking for much and most probably you will get a lot longer. If they agree to meet at the end of lunch time then maybe that is a sign that they aren't too keen for any extra time, however you never know, give them a shot, they may ask you back after school to finish the discussion - if not, try another teacher. Just remember, teaching a class of whatever age and size is a massive responsibility, you need to be focused all day - so pick your moment to ask a teacher for help wisely.

One important point to just keep in mind is that it is a working environment and all the people there are probably very busy and they don't owe you anything. So don't go in with the attitude that everyone is there to help you, crossing the line and coming across as annoying or needy will do you no favours. You could, if you were brave enough too, ask the head teacher or deputy head teacher for some of their time. But a word of warning they are often very busy people and your chances of success are slim, but then again you have nothing to lose. Try to catch them at a good moment and use some charm and who knows you may make a connection that sets you up for life!

Application and
Interview Advice

*"You can tell whether a man is clever
by his answers. You can tell whether
a man is wise by his questions."*

Naguib Mahfouz

Whichever Initial Teacher Education and Training (ITET)
route you take to becoming a primary school teacher, it
will inevitably result in you having to endure long form
filling out, experience a face-to-face interview and
possibly write a personal statement. This chapter
provides some guidance and suggests what you might be
asked. In the interests of fairness, and the fact that you
will want to stand out from the crowd, this chapter will
not be telling you exactly what to say or write in these
circumstances. Because if it did, then everyone who read
this may say or write the exact same thing and then no
one would be saying anything different - therefore no
one would be standing out.

However, this chapter will give you something better
than that. It will tell you about some important aspects
of primary school teaching. You should use these as a

starting point for your own research; this gives you a chance to make yourself stand out as everyone will have the opportunity to use their own initiative and research skills to develop their own understanding of modern day teaching and their own vision of themselves as teachers and their class as learners. There is also no guarantee that following this guidance will guarantee a place on a teacher training course or get you a teaching job as these results rely upon your personal qualities, experience and many other variables.

Aspects of Teaching to Consider

Behaviour Management:

Behaviour management is the ability to manage challenging or disruptive behaviour whilst also building and maintaining positive and mutually respectful relationships with your class, creating a learning environment that is conducive to outstanding progress and learning. This is achieved partly by creating and maintaining clear and consistent boundaries, fairness and by building positive relationships with the children; not as a friend, but as a teacher – you are the one calling the shots. If you don't have control of a challenging class, then the learning of the whole class will be hindered or even halted in extreme circumstances.

Engaging and Fun Lessons with Lots of Learning:

Your lessons should meet the needs of all the learners in the class and their respective ability ranges, as there may be quite a spread of abilities. You will extend the more able students and support the learning of those who find it harder to understand new concepts. Your lessons should ideally be very engaging and capture the imaginations of the children in your class. All the children should make outstanding progress.

Here are some other points to think about:

Accurate assessment and regular, personalised feedback and marking to all learners.

Good relationships with other staff and parents but especially with your own teaching assistant.

Well planned lessons that include differentiation.

An understanding of these acronyms EAL, SEN, FSM and Pupil Premium.

Subject knowledge.

Teaching strategies for learning.

Personal attributes and experience that make you the perfect candidate.

An important point to remember in any of these circumstances is to be child-focused. They are the most important thing about being a teacher and pretty much everything you do is to benefit them.

Personal Statements

The writing of a personal statement is a chance to differentiate yourself and show why you are an appropriate candidate to become a primary school teacher. You need to explain in detail why all your experience and personal attributes result in you being the perfect applicant for teacher training or the job in question. Including how you know working with children is suitable for you will be beneficial, as would an acknowledgement about the dedication involved in overcoming the challenges involved in becoming a primary school teacher.

Interview Advice

This section provides general interview advice that the more experienced of you may consider common sense, but it is necessary to include as not everyone has had the same life experience and many people will have got to this point in life without ever undertaking a formal interview.

1. **Do Your Research**
Whether it is researching a school, a university, a borough or just teaching in general make sure you are

fully aware of whatever it is you are getting yourself in for. One example of this could be reading a potential school's previous Ofsted report and mentioning the facts you learnt about the school in the interview. This will set you apart, show you are organised and show you are genuinely interested in the school. Just make sure that you are tactful if mentioning any areas of improvement!

2. Make a Good First Impression

It is amazing how many people timidly walk in to interviews avoiding eye contact and missing the vital opportunity to distinguish themselves and build a rapport with the interviewers. If you get this right, or even just do better than the last person, you will instantly set the interviewers perception off to a positive start. You must take the opportunity to make the slightest bit of small talk at the start, even if it about the weather, or how you are feeling, or how you were worried about being stuck in traffic despite you leaving extra early (perhaps dropping in how you travelled the route yesterday to make sure you knew it!) Another piece of advice is to pre-plan your handshake strategy! This may seem a little weird but it is advisable that you shouldn't instigate a handshake unless prompted to especially when you walk in. Perhaps as you leave may well be appropriate, but the interviewers will be leading the show here not you. One final point is that in all seriousness; do not go in for a kiss on the cheek as you depart. That is not appropriate interview behaviour.

3.   Have Two or Three Stories Ready to Relate Questions to

This is a great tip that will enable you to answer tricky questions with greater ease. If you are in an interview and the interviewer asks you to give an example of a time you used your initiative, it will probably be quite hard to wrack your brain for an anecdote or story that shows you off in a good light. Having two or three well known stories of examples of your previous successes or experiences from a work based scenario, that you can relate the questions too, will enable you to give better answers more quickly that show off your talents in a far more impressive way. Just make sure that you don't keep using the same story for every question.

4.   Don't Put Too Much Pressure on Yourself

You are judged mostly on your answers and the way in which you say them. You do not need to have given perfect answers. You just need to have given better ones than the other candidates! If you are nervous then you must have faith and trust in: yourself, your knowledge and the preparations that you have made and just remember that you don't need to be perfect - just better than everyone else.

5.   Dress Appropriately

You must dress appropriately for the job or role you are applying for and dress smartly so that you impress the interviewers. Turning up in anything less than smart formal clothes will instantly give off the wrong impression and adversely affect the way in which you are perceived.

Questions You May Be Asked

It is impossible to say exactly what you will be asked to write on any form, or answer in any interview, for a course or teaching job. It depends too much on what the interview is for, who is conducting it and even where in the country is it happening. This section will give you an outline of the sort of questions that are likely to be asked and the basic outline of what they will be trying to glean from you.

The interviewers are likely to be trying to build up a picture of you and your understanding of being a primary school teacher. They may want to know your views and opinions on teaching, learning, and whatever is happening in the wider world of education in the U.K. They will be trying to assess you as a person and your personal qualities and interests. They will be trying to ascertain your opinions on certain things that may be controversial, weighing up your values as a person and a teacher. They may well be figuring out your commitment, your motivation and your level of dedication.

Questions that may be asked, especially for teacher training, could include:

Why do you want to be a teacher?

What experience do you have and what has it taught you?

What is the role of the teacher?

What qualities make an outstanding teacher?

What would a good classroom look like?

Tell us what you know about differentiation

Talk to us about learning

Tell us about what you know about assessment

For an actual teaching job the question may well be more specific, like, give us an example of how you have used assessment for learning to improve your teaching, or talk to us about the role of data in assessment. You will also be required in most cases to actually teach a lesson to a class that will be observed. For a teacher training course you may even be required to give a presentation or work with a group of children.

The Importance of a Consistent, Caring and Understanding Role Model

"One looks back with appreciation to the brilliant teachers, but with gratitude to those who touched our human feelings. The curriculum is so much necessary raw material, but warmth is the vital element for the growing plant and for the soul of the child."

Carl Jung

You are needed. There is a vital role you for you to play in some people's lives. These people may only currently be toddlers, babies or not yet even born. But sometime in the future your paths will cross and you will have a special positive impact on their life. They, or you may never fully understand the significance, but you will have made a difference.

Sound like soppy nonsense to you? Well it isn't.

The harsh truth is that in today's society there are many children who have less than ideal role models in their lives or have seemingly bypassed the development of certain life skills. It is of course up to each parent how they raise their children. But some parents, for whatever reason, do not place such a high value or are unaware of how to develop certain personal attributes, which contribute to creating a child or young person that can operate successfully in the wider world. By modelling, demonstrating and explicitly teaching these behaviours and values you can make a difference to the future of that individual and help them to make more positive contribution to society.

One example of this could be something as simple as manners. A child could, for whatever reason: display poor manners, never saying please or thank-you; push, when they should be queuing or maybe they never learnt to share and always grab other people's things. By helping them to understand the importance we place in society on these small gestures and how it can affect how you are perceived. Another example could be certain social skills. A child may have parents who are very intellectually advanced and place high value on academic success, but are unaware themselves of the value of, or how to develop, certain emotional or social skills. The child may need a helping hand from you to enhance their friendship or communication skills or even to develop an understanding of their emotions. By showing compassion and awareness you have the unique opportunity to really make a difference to other human beings and give them a gift that will keep on giving for the rest of their lives. Think what a difference better communication and friendship skills could do for a child who struggles with those things. After all, you may spend more time in the week with these children than their parents do.

Many mothers these days have either decided or had it decided for them (for financial reasons) that they must work full time during the week. Historically this was not the norm. Consequently there are many children who do not see their mothers as often as they would like and need to receive at least some of that nurturing from elsewhere. There are also children who do not even have a mother figure in their lives or one that is less than perfect. These children, more than all others, will need to see a consistent, caring and understanding role model from which they can draw emotional strength from. Sadly, for some children school can be a sanctuary from the dysfunctional reality of their home lives. It is these vulnerable and unfortunate children who will need to receive and appreciate some consistency in their lives more than anything. Childhood should be a magical and wonderful time. Being at school in your class could be one of the warmest and happiest memories of another human being's life.

Overview of the Practical Elements of the Job

> *"The mediocre teacher tells. The good teacher explains. The superior teacher demonstrates. The great teacher inspires."*
>
> William A. Ward

This chapter is intended to give you a broad overview of the main elements of what the job actually entails. This will help you to build up a picture of the reality of the job and serve as a valuable reference point for when you actually begin your training and teaching. There is more detail to consider for each section, but it is not necessary to tell you at this point in your journey.

Planning

Planning is a very important part of the job. It enables you to be fully prepared to teach your lessons well and to make sure that there is a longer term direction and progression between each individual lesson. Planning involves looking at what is to be taught and how. This usually involves looking at the long term and the short term. For example your medium term plan will be an overview of what you are going to teach in each term, this plan enables you to break down the learning into steps that progressively expand the knowledge of each subject. Your weekly and daily plans will be looking at exactly how you plan to deliver each lesson.

Planning is a highly personal exercise that should be done in a way that is best suited to each teacher. There are many different ways to approach planning, some schools even have set plans already completed that each teacher must strictly adhere to each year. One of the benefits of this is that the teachers do not have to do much planning at all. The down-side is that there is little room for creativity, flexibility, spontaneity or variety for the teachers.

At first it can seem like there is a lot a preparation to be done and some new teachers can find that overwhelming. But it does get a lot easier over time. Thanks to the internet there are now many resources which aid the planning process by providing ideas or even offering ready made plans for a term's unit of work, for example, P.E planning for a six week period. You could download all of your planning if you were dedicated enough to finding it, but we wouldn't recommend it as it is better to come up with your own ideas that will excite you and make you more enthusiastic about the lessons. It can be beneficial to plan with a like-minded teacher, so that you can collaborate creatively and bounce ideas back and forth. As a new teacher this would also help you to get ideas and pick up planning tips.

The last point about planning is that you can plan a lesson to the point of excess, spending hours detailing every last exactitude and covering every imaginable thing you think will make an outstanding lesson and it could be a total flop, a real stinker. By the same token you can also make up a lesson, on the spur of the moment, which captures all their imaginations and from which masses of valuable information are retained the whole class.

Teaching

Once you have prepared to teach your lessons and have organised everything you need to communicate your objective in an engaging and successful way, it is time to deliver. The lion's share of your day involves teaching the children, working with them to expand their understanding of a wide variety of subjects. Many books containing millions of words have been written about teaching, and we're not about to tell you how to deliver a lesson, this is not the point of this book. The blog on our website is dedicated to providing tips for teachers of all levels of experience, as well as discussing all associated issues around the subject of becoming a primary school teacher and educating young people.

Differentiation

Your planning will enable you to meet the various needs of the children in your class, whose learning abilities will vary. This is called differentiation. This could be thought of as pitching your lesson so that all the children find the learning accessible and the more able students have their learning extended, whilst the less able have support provided to ensure they also achieve the lesson's objective on some level. Differentiation is something that you need to be aware of but don't worry if at first this seems a little daunting. It can take a year or two to fully develop your skills in differentiation, but an awareness of it is essential.

Assessment

This component of the job is very important as it helps you to: understand your class, inform them of how well they are doing and identify specific areas that they need to improve on to move them on to the next step in their learning journey.

Assessment, like planning, takes form in the short term and the long term. For example, the short term could involve checking the children's books after a maths lesson. This can help to identify any children who haven't really understood the learning. This informs your next day's planning as you can provide them with extra help. This is a logical way to teach a class if you think about it!

An example of longer term assessment involves checking the children's progress over a half term, whole term or even year. This is more suitable to get an overview and see how well they have retained the teaching from a longer period of time. This could take the form of a longer written maths test, or by setting unaided writing tasks that you then closely inspect to see how they have improved, whilst also identifying the next steps in their learning.

Accurate assessment is vital for teachers in many different ways, however to become accurate takes time and a real commitment to learning the skill. This commitment is a worthwhile investment as it will enable you to draw conclusions more quickly in the future and save you time when assessing at the end of each term (or half term if you have to).

Assessing writing, for example, is a difficult thing to do and can be a mentally strenuous procedure. Getting acquainted with the differences between each level and sub-level (whilst they still formally exist!) as quickly as you can, will reap you benefits in the long run. As time goes on you will be able to glance at a piece of writing and instantly level it intuitively, just having to refine it down to a more accurate sub-level.

Feedback and Marking

Feedback can take a variety of forms. We all remember having our books marked by the teacher, but this is only one way that children can get feedback on how they have done. You can also offer immediate verbal feedback throughout the lesson or soon after. This works well with all students but especially the more able members of the class.

Children can generate their own feedback by assessing their work themselves on how well they think have done. This can also be performed with a partner and is called peer assessment. Peer and self-assessment are a good way to get children to become more aware of themselves as learners, how well they are learning and what they need to do to move forward. In fact, the process of assessing with a partner enables children to explain what's being taught to each other which serves the benefit of solidifying what's been taught by the explainer, and clarifying something that may have been misunderstood by the child receiving the feedback.

Some say that teachers must mark every piece of work and provide feedback to the class in this way. This system can work fine, if children are given the time to understand the feedback, respond and discuss. But the question really is, does this always work and is it a wise investment of time? Children aren't robots that receive and assimilate every piece of written feedback neatly integrating it into a system of self-improvement. This is one reason why the received wisdom of feedback and marking must be questioned, as if there is no impact on progress and learning then the massive investment of time should be better used elsewhere.

Marking, and the close inspection of books by senior management teams and Ofsted inspectors, have recently become common place in primary schools. This hasn't always been such a high priority and new teachers coming into the profession should expect to receive clearly defined marking policies and procedures that are consistent throughout a school. As a new teacher you would be expected to mark the books to these standards consistently.

Every school is different, to a certain degree, but a good rule of thumb is that you would be expected to identify what has been done successfully, whether the learning objective was met or perhaps whether a target had been achieved. You would be required to identify the next steps in the child's learning journey or highlight specific areas for improvement in the work. You are also likely to be encouraged to ask questions and open a dialogue with individual pupils through the marking that you do. Of course, this can be quite a challenge when working with younger children or children with certain Special Educational Needs (SEN) who find reading and writing quite hard. In this case, you may find symbols are used to represent feedback points.

Schools are coming up with lots of innovative ways to provide accurate and meaningful feedback to their learners. There are many different strategies used and there is no "one size fits all" solution. You may encounter systems involving highlighter pens, a vast array of symbols, stickers or even computer based feedback systems. Whatever system you have to use, it is vital that you do not lose sight of the purpose of the feedback and make sure you give children the time to fully understand the marking you have done.

As you can probably tell, planning, marking and assessment take time to do well. Like everything in teaching it gets a lot easier and quicker with more experience - especially if you commit to reducing the time spent on these tasks. Qualified teachers are entitled to 10% of their working time for planning, preparation and assessment (PPA time) whether you actually get that or not depends on the head teacher. The time really benefits the children, so if you feel like you're getting stitched up, speak up for yourself!

If you require more information on any of these aspects of teaching and how they need to be combined together, then we have a product available from www.tes.co.uk (The Times Educational Supplement) called Effective Primary School Teaching Made Easy: Do What Works From The Start. It has been designed to follow on from this book and rapidly accelerate the process of becoming an outstanding teacher.

Learning

"The important thing is not so much that every child should be taught, as that every child should be given the wish to learn."

John Lubbock

As a primary school teacher you must have in the forefront of your mind an understanding of learning, however, learning is in many ways a mysterious beast. Before delving into the mysteries of the beast you should first consider these questions. How much do you actually think about learning? How much do you think about how people learn? And how aware are you about how you learn effectively as an individual?

As a teacher you are in the business of learning. Teaching is fundamentally about learning – enabling learning to happen. This fact can be forgotten at the expense of teaching, because to become a teacher you must first LEARN a lot of information before you are unleashed on a class and it is a steep learning curve. Understanding how you learn is vital. It will give you an understanding of yourself that will enable you to develop incredibly quickly as a teacher, and as a person, paying dividends to your career and your life.

It will also give you insights into the receptive learning experience of the children which you are vying to imbue with as much learning as possible. Children's learning is in many ways an enigmatic creature, almost esoteric in nature, but there are a few basic factors that you must be aware of as you develop your understanding of learning and the contexts it happens in.

Firstly, relevance to life experience. If you can communicate the lesson's objective in a way that they children can relate to then you are on to a winner. A very simple way of explaining this would be for example if you were learning about temperature and different states of water. You could get children to first explore various states of water that they might be familiar with, like asking have you ever seen your mum scrape her car on a cold morning or what is an ice lolly made of? Or have you seen something weird coming out of a boiling kettle? This just puts the learning in a context they can relate to and build upon their prior knowledge. Speaking of which...

The second consideration is their prior knowledge. Basically don't teach children to run before they can walk. A simple educational example would be you wouldn't try and teach a child how to include commas in their writing if they had no clue what a full stop is.

Learning skills and techniques often follows a linear progression.

The third basic facet of learning is repetition. In order for minds to grasp certain things, they need repetition or practice. Practice makes perfect. The repetitive nature of repeatedly doing a task helps the brain to form strong and lasting links within itself and solidify the acquisition of the new skill or piece of information.

The fourth consideration centres around what is called learning styles. There is much debate around this so you will need to do your own research and come to your own conclusions, but it is interesting to think about yourself what your preferred or most effective method of learning is. Knowing it will help you to become more self-aware and give you an advantage for when you begin your training. Chances are you won't fit neatly into one category but learning how you learn best can only be a good thing. Basically the theory is that that there are three styles of learning: visual, auditory and kinaesthetic. It is to do with how an individual experiences, ingests and remembers new information. A visual learner will prefer, and learn better, from receiving new information from a visual source, i.e. through their eyes. Auditory pertains to through your ears and kinaesthetic involves getting stuck in with your hands and getting involved for yourself.

These last four aspects of learning are vital and will give you an edge as a teacher and a learner. But there are more mysterious aspects to the workings of a child's brain; it can be quite an enigma. But there is one absolutely essential piece of information that many teachers under value in importance that underpins all aspects of learning and school life.

Perhaps you remember sitting in a particularly boring lecture or class, once upon a time in your past. You may remember the instance, the doodles you drew or the daydream you enjoyed whilst gazing out of the window or the wrong choice behaviour of certain individuals in the room, but we would be surprised if you remember the specific information that you were being expected to understand and remember. Your attention wandered because you weren't engaged, excited or interested in the subject, because it wasn't presented to you in an interesting, humourous or thoughtful way.

We would bet that when you cast your mind back to that boring lecture or class that possibly your last memory before drifting off into your own little world was of an individual entrusted with your education waffling on or reading a PowerPoint about whatever the subject was. Compare this to an experience that left you buzzing with the knowledge you had retained, we have all had them. You may have read a book, watched a documentary, experienced a lecture or been taken on a learning journey through knowledge by someone who managed to excite you. The difference is you cared. You remembered and learned because you cared. You wanted to learn and feed your mind because you were interested.

You see the point is that as adults we can make learning enjoyable for ourselves because we can identify how we learn best, what methods help us to retain information and also choose what we want to learn about and by choosing we are naturally engaged and we naturally care about it thus we remember. Children aren't able to do this by and large; so you have a choice. You can be the waffling ignoramus in front of class more concerned with what they are doing rather than their subjects. Or you can consciously choose to be someone who puts enjoyment and engagement at the heart of everything they try and teach.

Teaching, Understanding and Engaging Boys

> *"If a doctor, lawyer, or dentist had 40 people in his office at one time, all of whom had different needs, and some of whom didn't want to be there and were causing trouble, and the doctor, lawyer, or dentist, without assistance, had to treat them all with professional excellence for nine months, then he might have some conception of the classroom teacher's job."*

Donald D. Quinn

Whichever gender you are, you naturally gravitate your delivery of lessons and learning ideas, towards methods more attuned to that gender's preference. It is natural to come up with ideas for lessons that, you yourself would have found appealing as a child. The problem with this is that can be a contributing factor that can affect boys' engagement with their education, when the work being set has been thought up by a female.

Boys will typically represent half of your class, yet it may feel like more, as usually they are louder and more likely to create disruption and behavioural problems for teachers. It is for this reason that having a good understanding of how to relate to them, control them and engage them, is paramount to running a successful class. By consciously gearing work towards more "boy orientated" topics or their current interests, you will instantly engage them with the learning. Obviously a balance must be struck, but what you will probably find is that the girls will be more enthusiastic about undertaking boy focused work than the other way round. Apart from the ideas that generate the inputs and work of your lessons another crucial factor is behaviour management.

Behaviour management is a huge, complex yet subtle area of teaching that will be covered in depth in future support material from The Future Teacher Foundation. The subject covers controlling, motivating and building relations with a class and does require a set of skills to be developed. It is too in-depth to be delved into in this book. But this book will provide you with a basic idea of the importance of behaviour management in relation to the boys in your class.

Typically most of the disruptive or wrong choice behaviour will be from boys. That is not to say every girl you will teach will be an angel. But it is widely known that boys generally pose a greater challenge in this area.

You may have a class full of wonderfully behaved boys, but if you don't then you must not commit the cardinal sin of under-valuing the importance of excellent behaviour management skills.

Developing these should be your number one priority as a new teacher as you cannot teach if you don't have control. You must balance control, consistency, consequences, fairness, fun and relationship building, whilst outlining and sticking to clear boundaries so everyone knows where they stand and there is no confusion. Keep it simple. You will have your boundaries constantly tested so know what you consider to be acceptable and stick to it, but be realistic with your expectations or you will be setting yourself up for a fall.

Another aspect of understanding boys is to be aware of their innate need to play rough-and-tumble style games in the playground. They may seem like they are fighting or making wrong choices but for them, playing like this is something that just comes with being a boy (for most boys at some stage in their childhood). Obviously you should use your judgement but just be aware of this need as it does offer an insight into what's going on inside their heads. Failing to understand boys and what is important to them has made many a teacher come unstuck. By respecting them and being aware of the importance of engaging them, building mutual respect and controlling them well you will set your career off in the right direction.

Negotiating the Female Dominated Working Environment

"You can make more friends in two months by becoming really interested in other people than you can in two years by trying to get other people interested in you."

Dale Carnegie

It is likely that any primary school you enter will be female dominated. This gender imbalance can create interesting dynamics and situations that you must be aware of in order to flourish professionally. These circumstances are not always prevalent in primary schools, but it definitely pays to be socially smart, and aware of this intriguing aspect of primary school life.

Working in a female dominated environment can be very different to an evenly split gender workplace and very different to working in a male dominated one, so think carefully about your previous work or life experience and consider the male to female ratios you have previously encountered. Perhaps you may have worked in a clothes shop, for example, and have already experienced the female dominated workplace first-hand and are aware of the differences. The honest truth is that there **may** be an increased amount of "bitchy" behaviour. This phenomenon is amplified in the primary school environment. Schools can be very close knit and quite "full-on" in an emotional and stressful way. These factors do not bring out anyone's best side. Consider this example and heed its advice in order to make an intelligent and positive start to your life in a primary school.

New to a School

You will most probably arrive new to a school and completely unaware of the personalities, dynamic and history of the staff there. It could be a small village infant school or a huge inner city academy, the size doesn't matter. Whatever the type of educational establishment, there will be quite a few adults possessing a wide range of personalities and outlooks on life. You will likely be having professional contact with types of people you have never encountered (or just managed to successfully avoid!) from different generations, cultures and walks of life. You will make some great friends that you may keep for the rest of your life, but you will also possibly encounter some challenging individuals. But as it stands you go into this situation effectively blind – you know no one.

Your mission, of course, is to make a good first impression whilst subtly working out the dynamic. This takes time. So don't stress yourself out about making a huge impact on everyone immediately and figuring out how everyone relates to each other. These relationship dynamics may well be very subtle and complex and developed over many years. And making a first impression is also a gradual process built up over time, in this scenario. You must simply: smile, make eye contact, be polite and be interested in what other people are saying whilst you discretely monitor: seating arrangements, people's interactions, their closeness and any different cliques or factions within the staff.

Remember this is a worst case scenario, chances are everyone will be lovely, but it pays to be smart and not to "dive in too quickly" in a social sense. As we mentioned, staff at the school could have been there for years. There may be: cliques, factions, old enemies, gossips, stirrers, life-long friends or people you should just avoid. But of course like we say most people will likely be absolutely lovely individuals, but until you can build up a secure enough friendship to discretely inquire (with a trusted ally) into anything untoward you may have observed, hold back as you may be talking to someone who will go straight back to that person and tell them everything. Believe us, if someone's behaviour has come to your attention then you can be sure someone else there has noticed it too! Some people may object to this information being included in this book, please remember that this book is written for everyone and this advice may not be obvious to all. The intention of this book is to prepare <u>everyone</u> for the best possible start to their teaching careers.

How Problems May Arise

A day in a primary school can be physically and emotionally draining for a wide variety of reasons. This can lead to many issues as people don't always make right choices in these states of mind. If issues are caused by someone else, which does happen as you work in such close quarters, then some people tend to hold on rather than confront about the issue. If this happens it isn't easily forgotten and enemies can fester.

You could even be encouraged to join in any bitchy conversations, which could actually be quite bonding and therapeutic with like-minded individuals although we wouldn't necessarily recommend it. The truth is some people out there working in education aren't nice or professional, and their behaviour isn't conducive to a well-run school, and this can annoy you, especially if you take pride in doing your job well and you do need to vent these frustrations rather than bottle them up. Sound advice to politely negotiate these situations if you're not sure what to do, is to have stock phrases up your sleeve like "have you thought about telling her/him that?" or "well I don't really know her/him" or "no I hadn't noticed her/him doing that".

The most likely eventuality is that you will work in a school where everyone is kind and lovely, but whatever the mix of personalities it pays to not be naïve and to tread carefully when you first arrive.

The Importance of Communication and People Skills

"The most basic of all human needs is the need to understand and be understood."

Ralph Nichols

This chapter is the most important of all. This chapter underpins everything else in this book. By taking in the message that lies in what you are about to read, you will have instantly given yourself a major advantage to your career and your future.

Good communication and people skills are a vital part of successful teaching and working in a primary school. Firstly, a very large part of the actual teaching involves making sure your lessons are taught in a way that is understandable and accessible to all the children. This will be fairly obvious to most people contemplating teaching as a profession. What may not be so obvious is the importance of possessing good communication and people skills and using them to create positive relationships with the wide variety of people you will encounter throughout your day. This is an area which many prospective (and current) teachers under-value in significance. Due to demanding and varied nature of teaching and learning to teach, you will need to collaborate, co-exist and ask favours of your colleagues, so having them onside is a major advantage.

A typical day in a primary school could involve hundreds of interactions with a wide variety of people, ensuring that you have listened carefully and understood, and that you have communicated your point successfully will go a very long way to ensuring success in your endeavours. On any given day you may well have interactions with any number of: teaching assistants (TA's), special educational needs learning support assistants, other teachers, other teacher's TA's, your line manager, key stage co-ordinator or deputy head, the head teacher, the bursar, other office staff, the special educational needs co-ordinator (SENCO), the cleaner, lunch-time supervisor, emotional literacy support assistant (ELSA) or any other un-paid school support. You may also have to speak to external professionals like educational psychologists, speech and language therapists or autistic spectrum disorder outreach workers to name but a few, and finally any person who may pick up a child from school. This could include parents, grandparents, aunties, uncles, cousins, siblings, child minders, afterschool club workers, foster parents and neighbours, bearing in mind any of the above could come from all walks of life. Are you starting to see the significance of sound communication skills?

Let's look at two fictitious examples that illustrate this point:

Teacher A: Miss Taykes

Miss Taykes begins her day by not saying hello to anybody in the school, why bother, who cares? Once the children are in she begins berating them on what they haven't done also reminding them of how useless they are (failing to see the link between her behaviour and their lack of it) before they set off with their self-esteem damaged towards assembly, a lovely start to the day.

Mrs McGinty the TA arrives, with no greeting and showing zero interest in her life Miss Taykes proceeds to dictate her plans for the day showing no consideration for her strengths, likes or opinions. She tosses the TA instruction book towards her and she reads the demeaning, patronising text making her feel only slightly more intelligent, but less professionally respected, than a circus chimp. Consequently Mrs McGinty doesn't care about Miss Taykes' plans, bad mouths her constantly behind her back and also puts in less effort everyday taking any opportunity to undermine her. In fact she is thinking of quitting the profession, which is a shame because she has the potential to be an excellent teaching assistant.

Luckily for Miss Taykes, Mrs McGinty is at least a nice lady, because if she wanted to, she could make her life in class very difficult, very quickly. Miss Taykes continues through her day speaking with no thought considered for her audience leaving the children in her class bewildered and demotivated leading to very disruptive behaviour.

When engaging with other staff Miss Taykes is very keen to talk about herself and her class and can always be relied upon to always bring the conversation back to her and how great she is and how she has done whatever is being talked about but better. Actually this is a consequence of not feeling so great about herself but being unwilling to confront the inadequacy, in fact Miss Taykes is heading for a nervous breakdown as the consequences of her lack of people and social skills are starting to creep up on her from every angle. All the staff are whispering about her and laughing at her behind her back, no one wants to admit to being her friend and there is reluctance to help her in any way. The parents have turned on her too and are regularly coming to see her (and her superiors) with complaints and questions, which are obviously handled with a complete absence of any tact, sympathy or diplomacy. She is becoming completely alienated with no allies in or outside the class and even the management are rapidly losing patience with her. She spends her working life fighting to teach her class, being laughed at behind her back and trying in vain to stem the tide of problems that are coming at her from every angle. Her working day is becoming a living nightmare.

Compare this to teacher B: Mrs Wright-Choice

Mrs Wright-Choice begins her day by warmly greeting everyone she encounters with a smile and a chirpy hello, engaging in some small talk and showing an interest in other people's lives. She welcomes the children when they arrive and reaps the benefit of the mutually respective and trusting environment she has carefully created through listening to the children, communicating in a way they can understand and involving the children in dictating the direction of the learning journey. Feeling valued and safe, the children make their way sensibly to assembly.

Mrs McGinty arrives and is greeted by her first name Susan, enquiries are made as to how she is and questions are asked about her two children and how their swimming practice went last night, building on the good working relationship and friendship that the two have created. Mrs Wright-Choice outlines the course of the day and how they are going to work together to achieve the objectives, asking for her input and suggestions wherever appropriate leaving her feeling valued and empowered to take a significant role in the running of the class. They discuss ideas for a P.E lesson, as Mrs

105

Wright-Choice knows Mrs McGinty used to be a keen netball player and has a lot to offer the children in sports lessons. They agree for her to run a section of the lesson, which she is very keen to do so, and has many ideas to enhance the session.

This is a good start to the day and Mrs McGinty feels very happy about her work and is looking forward to doing the best job possible and supporting Mrs Wright-Choice in any way she can. Mrs Wright-Choice then proceeds through her day interacting successfully with the other adults and enhancing her reputation within the school with every person she communicates with. She listens, builds rapport and shows an interest in other people's lives and their classes creating a good reputation with the other adults, she is still discussed but only in positive ways and everyone is of the opinion that she will one day go on and become an excellent head teacher of her own school.

The day comes to an end and a notorious parent comes to speak to Mrs Wright-Choice about a very minor incident that their child has reported to them. This is clearly important to the parent and their emotions are running high. Mrs Wright-Choice listens to their points carefully and sympathetically, making them feel important and letting them let off some steam whilst not taking their comments personally. She then professionally, yet assertively, outlines her perspective on the events and agrees to investigate the child's claims further tomorrow arranging another quick meeting for feedback. The parent feels they have been heard and that something is being done and that Mrs Wright-Choice respects them, even if secretly Mrs Wright-Choice thinks they are a complete imbecile.

These are clearly two extreme examples but the point is exemplified. There are direct consequences linked to how you conduct yourself within the Primary school environment. Overlooking and undervaluing how you interact with people will create problems.

If you suspect this is an area for development for you then set about improving these skills. It is easily done, all it takes is a little bit of a commitment and you can save yourself a lot of problems in the long run. Even if you think you already possess good communication skills it still wouldn't hurt to brush up, considering the massive significance of these in this job. One book that will definitely improve these skills, is the self-improvement classic "how to win friends and influence people" by Dale Carnegie, this book is a good place to start to raise your social adaptability level and give you confidence and certainty in your interactions.

The truth is that dealing with people can be one of the most challenging aspects of teaching. Whether it be the behaviour management of a class, a difficult child, an awkward colleague or an uncooperative parent, skills which enable you to understand and effectively deal

107

with people will help you immensely. The problem can be with parents is that they can sometimes see themselves as customers. If you have ever seen or dealt with an angry customer, or been one yourself, imagine if you were angry about a problem that involved the most precious thing in your whole life. Your child. Some parents even have issues with schools or institutions from their previous life experience that exacerbate these problems further. Another factor to consider is they may have been stewing all day on a grievance, planning what to say and imagining every angle and they suddenly spring it on you after a busy day at work. They are prepared and they know to pounce on you at your most vulnerable. Don't be afraid, look forward to the challenge and learn skills and techniques for effectively dealing with people. Believe us, you will thank us one day.

Observing and Being Observed

"To acquire knowledge, one must study; but to acquire wisdom, one must observe."

Marilyn Vos Savant

When you begin your teacher training, or when you first get into a school, make sure you go out of your way to observe experienced teachers. Observing experienced teachers is one of the best ways to learn your craft in the early stages. So much can be gleaned from analysing the teaching of someone else. Obviously, the better the quality of teacher you observe, the more you will learn, and the higher quality of their teaching practice will mean that you are getting the best input from the start - so it is prudent to choose your victim wisely. That said, you can learn what not to do from less able teachers but at the start it can be hard to tell their quality, as your frame of reference may be small. Either way, all teaching professionals should have things to teach you - we would hope!

So what should a trainee or new teacher be looking out for in initial observations of primary school teachers? Well, it is a good idea to focus observations quite tightly at the beginning. However sometimes it is better to keep an open mind and just see what happens in the lesson and what tips and ideas you can steal. Once you do this, and you observe a really good teacher in action, you will probably end up with cramp in your hand from all the notes you will be taking from watching a master in full flow. If you have found someone like this and you have access to them, then we would advise that you "milk that cow" for all it's worth – without becoming a nuisance or a burden. The mentor you have been allocated *may* not be the best teacher in the school, teachers can vary in quality a lot, this is a fact that we can pretend isn't true - but it really is. There can a humungous difference between an average or poor teacher and an outstanding one, so if you have access to an outstanding one, make them your friend!

Aspects of teaching that you may consider, should be linked to your areas of development or immediate learning needs, for example, behaviour management. This crucial aspect of teaching is one of the first things you will need to work on. Other aspects could include: specific teaching techniques, groupings, differentiation and ability matching, learning objectives and how they are met or the use of other adults in the class - to name but a few. Don't worry if this is too daunting and it all seems a bit much, it gets a lot easier over time.

Being Observed

Lesson observations at any stage of your teaching career can be a nail-biting experience. Whether it's a regular lesson whilst training, a final assessment observation, a performance management observation by a head teacher, a parents in school day or the dreaded Ofsted inspector - the idea that someone is scrutinising your performance can be a very worrisome ordeal.

The nerves often come from feeling like you aren't prepared enough, even though you may have spent hours in preparation! If this is the case then a great tip is to take a minute or two to have faith and trust in the preparations you have made and just go for it.

Throughout the early stages of your career when learning how to become a primary school teacher, feedback is essential from an experienced practitioner after the lesson observation. Hopefully that person will have no ulterior motive other than having your best interests at heart. By this we mean that people are fallible and we all have insecurities. Perhaps you may not be aware, but maybe your youthful exuberance, relationship with the class and clear potential could make someone feel threatened: sub-consciously or not. If you have an excellent mentor, then consider yourself very fortunate as sadly that is not the case for every trainee teacher. Your mentor could be inexperienced in mentoring themselves, and this is also a factor to consider.

You should assess the quality of the feedback you receive, and whether they have provided you with what you did well and what you could improve on for next time. If their suggestions for improvements are things you had identified already, then that is great for you: it is a good sign you are an honest and accurate reflective practitioner on the way to success. If you feel the feedback is consistently inadequate then maybe you need to be observed by someone exceeding your current mentor's abilities: to get a deeper insight into teaching and how you could improve.

Positives, Negatives and Dealing with Problems

"There is nothing either good or
bad but thinking makes it so."

William Shakespeare

There are no other jobs like primary school teaching. One minute you can be trying to get a hula-hoop down for a girl who has thrown it 10 feet up a tree, the next offering advice to a boy who trusts you and having a tough time at home, providing him with positive support he otherwise wouldn't have access to. From the insignificant to the very significant you never know what you are going to get in any day, but you can be sure that no two days will be the same. They cannot be due to the unpredictability of children and the way they respond to each other, adults and learning.

Time does go quickly during the school day, you will rarely be watching the clock down. That cannot be said for many jobs. And yes, you do get thirteen weeks paid holiday and yes, the six week summer holiday is truly excellent but the truth is you do need those half terms as much as the children do to recharge and rest your mind. You see like any job there are negatives. But in many cases it is down to your perception regarding how much you let them affect you. Here are a few of the negative comments you may hear from people and some suggestions to help counteract those experiences if you suffer them.

Teaching is a stressful and at times thankless task. Yes it can be, but you need to develop skills in time management and efficiency, also by getting to know yourself better and how you react to certain situations and stimuli will reduce the impact of "stressful" situations on yourself. You also need to learn to congratulate yourself on yours and the children's achievements as you may not get much appreciation from anywhere else.

You work with the threat of Ofsted hanging over your head and under a government that can appear to be unsympathetic and unsupportive of your role, who change aspects of your job without seeming to have fully thought it through and often without any academic research or evidence to back-up their decisions. This is often sadly true. The truth is about Ofsted that they are just quality assurance, if you are doing your job properly and have all your paperwork up to date, then you have nothing to worry about. They are mostly checking up on the bosses really! So you can see why some bosses need to put their stress onto their subordinates.

The workload is too much for the money. Well there can be some truth in this but it comes down to how organised you are, the management of the school and your personal time management and efficiency skills. You must think about the impact of the time you are putting in and how it will actually benefit the children. Some people like to spend their whole life planning and marking because that is their life and that's fine if that is what they want to do. The job expands to the amount of time you are willing to give to it. If you ever feel like the pressure or work is too much and there isn't enough time then you must stand up for yourself and take steps to retain the work life balance.

The pay is rubbish. Well, you start of at a certain point on the scale and progress is down to your performance. There are also many future career development opportunities and it is more acceptable to find women in the upper echelons of the school hierarchies compared to the private sector. Plus once you factor in the thirteen weeks of the year that the school is shut the picture looks even rosier.

The key thing is when you are training the task ahead will seem daunting. There is a lot to learn. But it is manageable. We think of it as climbing a mountain, you keep climbing and one day your knowledge gets to a critical mass and you get to a peak and you find that you are looking down at the mountain and surrounding landscape below and you feel on top of it all.

115

Appendix 1: The 50 Best Things about being a Primary School Teacher

The list is in no particular order. Some points have been referenced earlier in the book and are elaborated upon within. Teaching can be very hard. This list will help you to remember the positives when the going gets tough.

1. Inspiring Children and Changing the Course of their Lives

One of the most rewarding things you can do as a primary school teacher is to inspire a child in a way that you can see will significantly help their current and future life. As an adult working with children you will have the opportunity to see their lives with a clarity that they themselves do not possess.

As you get to know your class you will be able to identify needs that they have that you can enable them to fill. You could inspire a child to take part in sport, which would have benefits for their health, social interaction and self-esteem changing the course of their life forever. You could inspire a child to believe that they can be creative and are able to draw pictures, creating a lifelong passion for art. You could identify that a child who struggles with writing just needs more time and support to plan their work, once this has been fixed their creativity, ideas and writing talent is unleashed and they now believe that they can do it, giving them a platform to continue to build on so they can achieve their future potential.

These aspects of primary school teaching are very hard to measure but they are the really meaningful interventions that can truly change an individual's life forever.

2. Varied Opportunities for Promotions and Pay Rises

Many people believe that schools offer very limited opportunities for career progression. A common misconception is that the options are strictly limited to the teacher – deputy head – head teacher career path. This is not true; there are an ever increasing amount of roles that can add more responsibility to your working life and more money in your pay packet! Admittedly, the options may well be a bit more limited than working for a huge multi-national company – but there still are options.

Promotion opportunities include roles like subject leaders or curriculum co-ordinators, who oversee specific aspects of the curriculum. Key stage co-ordinators, who oversee, lead and manage specific age ranges. Special Education Needs Co-ordinators (abbreviated to SENCOs), assistant head teachers, early years co-ordinators and advanced skills teachers. Some schools may not have all of these and other roles could be created for specific needs. Academies have even more freedom to create management and leadership roles as they have more autonomy over how they spend their budgets.

3. The Moment when "the Penny Drops"

This highly rewarding aspect is something that can be achieved daily. Whether working with an individual, group or whole class you have the chance to make previously unknown information and concepts become understood creating a new connection with the mind that can last a lifetime. These rewarding moments should be treasured and are largely unique to teaching. They do not only just apply to traditional academic subjects or curriculum based learning but can also be applied to helping children to see the value of many social and emotional "life skills," such as the value of: listening, thinking before you speak, recognising negative emotions and coping with them, making and retaining friends and recognising an individual's strengths and what they can contribute to the world. And better yet you get the chance to do this every single working day.

4. Thirteen Weeks Paid Holiday Every Year

A Quarter of a year, 13 weeks, 91 days, 2184 hours...Whichever way you look at it, it is a very large amount of time to have to rest, enjoy yourself or prepare for your next term. If you are in full-time employment now, then chances are that you get far less holiday than this. You will need to watch out for possible envy from friends and family especially as the six week summer holiday approaches. The only reason they will ever be envious is just because they wish they had what you are about to receive. Six weeks off in the summer is truly luxurious and genuinely one of the best things about being a primary school teacher.

5 Recession Proof Job Security

The recent financial troubles of the globe have affected many sectors of the work force. Education in Britain, whilst not entirely unaffected, has come through so far relatively unscathed. Budgets have been ring-fenced and great swathes of teachers have not been laid off unable to pay their bills and mortgages. The future cannot be predicted, but the continued education of our young people is a priority for our society and the government continues to pump billions into our education system every year. These factors result in greater job security than many other jobs.

6. The Chance to Work within a Local Community

You may hear an idiot say that primary school teaching is not "working in the real world". Well, sorry idiot – but working in a local community building links with real people and enhancing the lives of the families in that community, is the real world. Primary schools are often the only real hubs of local communities where people come to meet up and access a surprisingly wide range of services.

There may well be schemes in place to help serve the local community by: building links with local businesses, working with emergency services, liaising with park rangers, litter picking or working with an old people's home to name but a few. Working within a community can bring a real sense of purpose, identity and pride in the value that you add to that area and the people who live in it.

7. Being a Positive Role Model for Young People

There aren't many jobs that enable you to have the chance to be "looked up to" by around 30 other people on a daily basis. You will be able to use the admiration you create as a force for good, by demonstrating and modelling positive behaviour to copy. This could be as simple as demonstrating good manners and courtesy to others. Or this could be something like promoting the value of knowledge and learning, that inspires an individual to see the world in a new way. A way that changes their attitude about learning from being something boring, difficult and unachievable to a realisation that the world is full of wonder and that learning about it is an enjoyable and achievable experience.

8. Getting to Enhance and Develop Children's Minds

The daily process of teaching and learning adds up to a long term cumulative effect on the minds and abilities of the children that you teach. Depending on the age of the children and what you are teaching them, progress in a lesson or over a day may be small, but these small incremental improvements add up to significant change over the course of a term or a school year.

You will get to enhance critical educational skills involving maths and English. This could involve finally getting a child to read fluently, unleashing their creativity and vocabulary in writing or solidifying the techniques within their mind that they require to solve a wide variety of mathematical problems. You could foster a scientific curiosity about the world that inspires children to learn independently outside of school just for the enjoyment and satisfaction they get about increasing their knowledge. You could be the one who exposes them to a new sport which grows into a lifelong passion. You could make them aware of new kinds of music, drama, dance and performance that broaden their cultural horizons. You could give them a deeper understanding of history, geography and religion that creates a wonder and curiosity which results in a lasting fascination and quest for truth. You could also make a significant contribution to helping many individuals become the best they can be by helping them to grow as people and develop the key skills that they need to move forward in their lives.

All of these opportunities to enhance and develop the minds of children can be achieved over the course of a school year resulting in lasting positive effects that have many wonderful repercussions throughout an individual's future.

9. Going on Days out on School Trips

A day out on a school trip can be a magical experience but it does depend on where you go, what you do there and who you are with. They always provide a great opportunity to learn outside the classroom environment and bond with your class, developing positive relationships that will continue back at school.

You may be surprised to learn that many tourist attractions can cater for school trips, this includes: zoos, theme parks, castles, aquariums, museums and parks. This means that every now and then you will get the chance for an all-expenses paid trip to somewhere fun! Well maybe not all expenses you'll probably have to buy your lunch. These trips out of school for the day will provide variety for you and the chance for your class to enhance their learning with real-life examples. If you are wondering how this can be applied to Alton Towers, well its science for starters, all of the rides use forces to move! Some establishments will even run the entire day for you as well with workshops, talks and practical activities.

Depending on the school, you may get to choose where you go on a class outing. Of course, the most important factor in choosing a destination is whatever location has the greatest benefit to the children's learning, but look a little harder and you will be able to also find somewhere that will be a great day out for everyone too. Chances are that you remember your best school trips from your primary age education. These days often provide lasting memories for the children so make sure that they won't forget your school trips for all the right reasons.

Taking a class of 32 children out into the world is a massive responsibility and one that can't be taken lightly. You will need to make sure you have risk assessments and be prepared for a day of constant head counting to make sure you bring back the same amount as you left school with!

10. Celebrations and Festivals

Times of the year like Christmas, Eid and Diwali are fun for everyone but especially for children. Whatever the religious background to the festivities or event, children always enjoy the excitement and fun that comes with these special times of year. Working with children around these times enables you to get involved with the joy and even celebrate new things that you previously had never gotten involved with.

Taking Christmas as an example, it is a wonderful thing to be able to talk to young children who celebrate Christmas about their Christmas experience and of course, Father Christmas, and see their faces light up as they describe their thoughts and understandings. Christmas time can also often provide variety in your working week too. If you are in a school where the majority of children celebrate Christmas then you may find that there may be carol concerts, Christingle services, church visits or even nativity plays to take part in. The days may be broken up with special Christmas activities and you may well be encouraged to base the children's learning around festive activities.

11. Making the World a Better Place Everyday

Working in a primary school environment enables you to make the world a better place every single day. It may not be much and the impact could just be small, but not every job provides this lovely opportunity. Of course this can be achieved by successful learning, promoting positive values and helping individuals and classes to develop. But also by spreading kind words and compliments to children, parents and other adults that you encounter. When it comes to making a difference, primary school teaching really does give you that opportunity to make others feel good every single day.

12. Working in a Small Team that is Part of a Larger Team

As a primary school teacher you could be working in class on your own all day – in this example you really are working in a small team! But chances are that you will have some support from other adults in the capacity of teaching assistants or other helpers. If this is the case, which is the more likely option, then you have the responsibility for leading and managing the team towards a shared objective, working closely together and succeeding together. This is great because it gives you the opportunity to get the best out of someone else and make their working life enjoyable and highly productive creating great team spirit.

You will also be working as part of a larger team that contains the whole school (the size and management structure of the school will dictate how much interaction you have with other members of staff) and your efforts will contribute to the bigger picture of the success of the school and its goals. This larger team will support you and offer advice if need be and you are likely to have the opportunity to contribute to discussions and suggest strategies that support the learning and day-to-day running of the school. Working in this way can provide a real sense of belonging and purpose in your life.

13. Getting to Help and Support Families in Need

As a teacher you are privileged to serve a community by educating the children and to an extent supporting the families. You will get to know lots of different families and they will get to know you too and there will be many opportunities throughout a year of working with their children to help them in professional ways by: supporting them through difficult times, advising them on how they can support their child's learning, noticing if their child is out of sorts and raising this concern to the parents but most of all making their child happy by your excellent and fun teaching - this is the best way to support families and the local community as it promotes greater well-being and harmony inside their own homes, and they will really appreciate you for it too.

14. Being involved in Sport, Music and Art

Many of you will have specific interests in these areas and already be looking forward to sharing your skills and knowledge with a class. Even if you think that you do not have anything to offer in these subject areas you might be surprised how they grow to become some of your favourite subjects to teach. You may find yourself looking forward to these lessons as they contribute to the overall picture of variety that is the life of a primary school teacher.

The chance to take your class out for some fresh air and a run around in structured sports activities, does them the world of good and contributes to class morale. This can also be used as an incentive to good behaviour. The same can be said for art and music too. Even if you or your teaching assistant don't feel you are "good" at art or music, you can still enjoy the lessons and take the opportunity to learn with the children. They will love this and it shows that you are brave enough to admit that you aren't perfect and that we all have different strengths and weaknesses.

Generally speaking, children love art lessons and the chance to be creative. Learning a few techniques with materials and incorporating art across the curriculum to all areas of learning, is a great way to get your class fully engaged in any subject. Once you have engagement and enjoyment you have enthusiasm and you have learning.

Many of you may well have sports you follow, music you like or art you appreciate. Any fondness you have for these areas can be related the curriculum with a bit of creativity. In doing this you will make your teaching more enthusiastic and your lessons better as a result. An example of this would be using your favourite songs when analysing and comparing music for rhythm, song structure or tempo. You could even expand this to look at song lyric writing (poetry) or to use the examples for dance lessons in P.E.

15. Sharing your Knowledge and Enthusiasm

If you have a love for learning, knowledge and all things academic then that is a great trait for a primary school teacher to have. Your enthusiasm for knowledge will shine through to your class and inspire them to learn. If general knowledge isn't your thing and you make excuses when trivial pursuit comes out, all you need to do is to find something that you find interesting about that subject and use that as a starting point for your teaching. Chances are that if you find it interesting then your class will too. Unless they are a particularly cynical bunch!

Every teacher has areas of the curriculum that are closer to their hearts than others - primary school teaching provides you with an opportunity to share this and possibly spark off an enthusiasm within someone else for thing that you love.

A great thing about primary school teaching is that you are in the role of the "expert" and it is your responsibility to share knowledge and you have a captive audience ready and waiting to listen to your wisdom.

16. Developing Yourself and Your Skills

Becoming a primary school teacher is a process of reflection and improvement that lasts a whole career. Primary school teaching provides you with a unique opportunity to better yourself and develop as a person. We are all learning, and no one is the finished article yet!

There may well be training you can attend, especially if you choose to progress your career towards leadership, that will enlighten you to many new ways of thinking and behaving that can help you to become a more successful, happy and complete person which will benefit every area of your life.

You will also improve on your skills in communicating and dealing with other people, as you have no choice but to be involved in social interactions on a daily basis. Every time you speak to a parent or colleague in a professional or social capacity you have an opportunity to reflect upon and improve on the success of the interaction so you can improve on the end result next time.

17. The Many Primary School Job Opportunities in the U.K

Once you have gained qualified teacher status (QTS) you can teach anywhere in England and Wales this means that you have the freedom to move around anywhere in these two countries, and have the potential to get a job in your area of expertise

If you gain qualified teacher status in England or Wales you can apply for the qualification to be recognised in other countries too, this applies also to the equivalent qualification gained in Scotland or Northern Ireland.

Whilst there is of course competition for jobs, it is also true to that primary schools and equivalent age teaching establishments are in every community across the whole country. This means that there are nearly 17,000 establishments that you are qualified to work in. In fact if you think about it that is possibly the most employment options offered by any degree level job. To put into context for you the sheer amount of primary age schools in the U.K - we all know that McDonalds and Starbucks are everywhere these days, well they only have around 2000 stores between them in the U.K!

18. Annual Events to Look Forward to like Sports Day and World Book Day

Schools each have their own traditions and different ways of doing things; you may well be surprised at the variety of events that take place over the year. Two events that are fairly consistent across the country are sports day and World Book Day. Many of you will remember your own sports day; you may find however, that it is a slightly different experience from an adult's perspective! There are many ways to run a sports day and some schools may even give it a different name, and watch out because you may be asked to run in a teacher's race!

World Book Day is a relatively new event that many schools take part in. Children are encouraged to dress up as their favourite book character and school's often spend the day focusing on reading and writing and celebrating all things to do with books. The World Book Day website also streams workshops and talks from popular authors and illustrators throughout the day for children to learn from.

19. The Fun of the Last Day of Term

Many of you will remember having fun in school on the last day of term from when you were small. Perhaps you were allowed to take in a board game or a toy? Many schools across the country still follow this age old tradition! Chances are that by the last day of term your class will be pretty tired, especially after all that learning and knowledge you have crammed into their brains!

So the last day of term may well be a fun day where games can be played and even parties may be held, you may even find that the school closes early too! If the school you eventually work in doesn't operate such a system then maybe you could suggest it? It is a great way to reward good behaviour and incentivise your class to be well behaved; the thought of a treat on the last day of school is often something they love to look forward to.

20. Good Maternity Leave

Whilst this won't apply to everyone, it is definitely one of the best things about being a primary school teacher for many potential and experienced primary school teachers. Typically, any teacher who has had a baby is entitled to 52 weeks maternity leave with 32 weeks of this being salaried – not full salary though sadly! You would probably receive 4 weeks full pay, 2 weeks 90%

pay, 12 weeks at 50% pay and the remaining 21 weeks on statutory maternity pay assuming you fulfil the criteria for eligibility, which you probably would. Whilst this may not be the best maternity package in the entire country is a lot better than many private sector packages.

21. Once a Teacher Always a Teacher

Upon gaining qualified teacher status, you are entitled to begin your newly qualified teacher induction period. Once this is completed you are officially a teacher. Forever. This cannot be taken away, unless there is a severe reason to do so, and you have the option at least, to work as a teacher for the rest of your working life.

This means that if you find after a few years that you want to try to pursue another lifelong dream or take time out to become a full-time parent, you can do so safe in the knowledge that you can return to teaching at any point. You may need to take some kind of refresher course in this instance, but teaching is like riding a bike, you never forget!

22. Opportunities to Work Abroad

As a fully qualified teacher you are a member of a profession that provides the unique opportunity to work abroad in many countries. This may not appeal to everyone right now, but it does mean that you have the option if there is a dramatic change in your living circumstances or if you have a mid-life crisis!

Seriously though, there are English schools for ex-pats in many countries and there is also the option to teach in regular schools in those countries too. Be aware that some qualifications like the PGCE, or School Direct aren't recognised by some country's governments, so if this is something you are seriously considering, do your research thoroughly.

23. Potential for Extra Income from Tutoring

You can earn a good hourly rate for tuition and depending on the area; you may be surprised at the demand for such a service. Typically maths and English are the usual subjects covered, but if you are in a grammar school area then many parents require tuition for their children so that they have a better chance of passing the 11-plus entrance exams.

Some tutors in London have been charging extortionate amounts for their services, so there is serious money to be made. If you live in or near an affluent area then this could be something that proves to be very lucrative for you. If you don't then do not despair, tutoring is needed all over the land and there may well be agencies or local websites that can help to put you in touch with potential clients. Tutoring not only provides extra financial income but also enables you to sharpen up your subject knowledge and explaining skills, whatever stage of teaching you are at.

24. You get to be as Creative as you Like

This is one of the best things about being a primary school teacher because you do not need to be creative to succeed at all. Being a creative person does provide an advantage. As a primary school teacher there are lots of problems to solve in planning and designing lessons and learning activities; having lots of ideas will make these processes easier. But nowadays, thanks to the internet, there are so many resources and websites dedicated to providing ideas, that if you struggle with coming up with ideas, there is lots of help available for you.

If however, you are a creative person and love coming up with ideas, then you will find that primary school teaching will enable you to flex all of your creative muscles and push your creativity to the max. It should also be said that if you do not consider yourself a creative person, then maybe you could decide to work on those skills? With a bit of effort any aspect of yourself can be improved upon, the investment in time will be worthwhile for the positive effects on your working life.

25. Planning Preparation and Assessment (PPA) Time

This applies to teachers who have finished their Newly Qualified Teacher (NQT) induction period. During the NQT induction period (otherwise known as the NQT year) you will have 20% of your time outside of the classroom. This is makes the top 50 as this allocated time has only come into being recently, in the past, teachers had to be in the classroom teaching all day every day.

Having a few hours, a morning or an afternoon to perform essential tasks really enhances your teaching practice and subsequently the learning and progress of your class. You may have heard stories about The Department for Education planning to scrap this time. Hopefully there is no substance to this story as scrapping PPA time will certainly have a detrimental effect on children's learning and on teacher morale.

26 Lots of Continuing Professional Development (CPD) Opportunities

This relates specifically to the opportunities to continually enhance your professional skills and knowledge through training. This may come from centralised training, workshops and lectures that are provided by the local authority that oversees the school you are in. They may also come from an independent advisory establishment (this is more likely if you work in an academy).

Wherever the training originates from, this is all paid for by the school and entrance to some of these courses for independent people outside of education, can cost hundreds of pounds a day. What this means is that you will be receiving access to high quality training and information to enhance your professional life for free!

27. Being the Teacher they Remember

You may well remember your favourite teacher from school and the way they made learning fun. You may just remember a piece of work that you were really proud of, or a specific lesson that captured your imagination, or how an adult was kind to you when you needed help. Surely you personally, want to leave a lasting positive impression with all the children that you teach.

Childhood should be a magical time and you can contribute to making someone's a little bit more special.

This aspect of the job is unfortunately hard to measure! You may well meet a former pupil in the distant future as they pull up next to you on their hoverboard telling you how they still remember being in your class and how you were their favourite teacher, but then again you may not. But the truth is that you will know by the way in which children respond to you, whether or not you have left a lasting positive impression. You'll just know. You shouldn't set out to be loved; that is a major wrong choice. But by being a great teacher, making learning fun and by treating each child in your class as an individual you will surely leave an impression that lasts for many years to come.

28. A Professional Status and Respect Comes with the Job

You will find that when you are a professional teacher you will attain a certain status within society (not quite as highly regarded as it should be but there you go!) and be on the receiving end of respect from other professionals that you meet because of it.

You will also get respect from intelligent people outside of the working environment who understand that primary school teaching is a highly valuable job in our society and how it can be a challenging job that definitely requires dedication and intelligence to master. There are certain sections of society who do not respect the job, those people should be referred to as idiots, and should be avoided at all costs!

29. The Chance to Earn and Maintain Respect in School

Being a teacher does come with a certain degree of kudos especially in the eyes of colleagues, pupils and parents who respect you. Respect of course needs to be earned through your professionalism, kindness and skill in doing your job to the best of your ability.

Inside the school environment the chance to earn respect from all the people who you encounter is a goal that can only be achieved over a longer period of time. This means that it is not easy but would be a real achievement if accomplished. This makes the list because you have the opportunity as a primary school teacher to be known by many people and to build a positive reputation for yourself amongst these people. Establishing yourself, gaining respect and cementing your reputation as a fantastic teacher shouldn't be your main concern when beginning teaching. If you do a great job and be nice to everyone then it will happen naturally.

30. The Amount of Help that is now Available from the Internet

The internet has been mentioned before in the context of creativity, but this is one of the best things about being a primary school teacher in 2014 for sure in its own right. Regardless of the plethora of planning and lesson ideas material that is out there, the internet has so much more to offer modern primary school teachers like:

- Social media and web forums that provide opportunities to keep up to date with new developments in education.
- Websites that stream or let you download videos enable you to bring all sorts of information into your lessons in engaging ways that capture children's imaginations.
- Games websites that help you to make learning fun and by using enjoyment to convey the lessons learning objectives.
- Information based websites that you can incorporate into your planning on practically every curriculum subject.
- Search engines enable you to access all the information in the world at your fingertips for impromptu lessons that develop from your class' curiosity.

- The ability to download resources and even complete lessons or units created by experienced teachers from sites like the TES and TeachersPayTeachers (which is based in the U.S).

31. Getting to Work and Interact with a Lot of Adults

This is meant in a social sense, as you may find that you are working in a school which actually has a lot of other adults working there too. Of course the amount will depend on the school's internal organisation and its size. You may be surprised when you realise how many people do actually work in the school that you find yourself in. You may well even discover that most of the other teachers or teaching assistants are of a similar age to you with similar interests, giving you the opportunity to make friends for life. Primary school teaching can be a very bonding experience with colleagues as you are all going through the same thing and will have lots in common to discuss; you may find you make close friends very quickly with your colleagues.

32. You get to Teach a Wide Variety of Subjects

The chance to teach the entire breadth of the national curriculum is a very appealing aspect of the job, and rightly deserves its place in the top 50 best things. This has a big impact on the overall variety of the job and the speed at which a day seems to pass by. Teaching in secondary school doesn't offer anywhere near the same variety as teaching younger children and if you are the sort of person who has a wide range of interests then surely you can't wait to have a go at teaching everything! You may be a little apprehensive about teaching certain subjects and that is perfectly normal. A great tip that we have mentioned before is to simply confess your ignorance and to learn with the children discovering new information together and sharing in the intrigue and wonder. It works magically as children love to complete a shared objective with adults.

33. You are in Charge of Your Very Own Class

Having your own class takes at least a year to achieve if you train through a postgraduate route; longer of course if you gain a degree that comes with QTS. But the privilege of having your own class enables you to put all your ideas and training into practice for real and do things your way, having complete control over the organisation and day-to-day running. This sense of pride, ownership and the responsibility that comes with it will give you a real sense of achievement, especially when you see the fruits of your labours paying off as the children make excellent progress under your expert guidance.

34 Flexibility in How you Teach

Depending on the school you work in and the style of the leadership and management there, you may well find that you have complete creative control over how you teach the class. Primary school teaching is such a vast and complicated job that there is no way that the teaching can be completely prescriptive. You will be allowed to use your judgement as a professional to make decisions about how best to teach the class and how to approach each subject to get the best results. Of course you will be guided through this process by your training, mentors and the school's leadership and management whose years of experience will provide you with valuable nuggets of information to aid you if you aren't sure.

Perhaps you might decide that a whole day needs to be dedicated to exploring a subject in a holistic way so that future lessons can be later fed from this huge day of learning. Maybe you think that going outside will inspire your class to learn about another lesson's objective. Perhaps you think that bringing in cooking ingredients and making a cake will inspire the right reaction in your class. Maybe you decide that the class needs a double length maths lesson to fully understand this new concept or that you will teach your English lessons in the afternoon as it works better. In the best and most open-minded of schools this will be encouraged.

35. Opportunities for Part-Time Work if Required

The majority of jobs often have little scope or opportunity for part-time work. It seems to be full-time or nothing. This is not the case when working as a primary school teacher. You may not feel like you have any need or desire right now for anything less than full-time work and that is great, but nobody knows what the future may hold. Being a primary school teacher opens you up to the possibilities of working part-time contracts that could be 0.4 or 0.6 of a week that still entitle you to be paid over the school holidays and give you PPA time.

You also have the option of doing supply teaching which could give you even greater flexibility. Supply teaching could also be an option for an income if you find yourself out of work for a period of time. When you consider being able to earn money through tuition too, you can see how being a primary school teacher lends itself well to wide variety of different employment options and lifestyle choices.

36 Gaining and Developing Transferable Skills

Learning to become a primary school teacher will be a test of your resourcefulness, intelligence and character. The process of learning the trade is a long one as the job is very complex. There is an often held misconception about the job that it must be easy to do, as you are "only teaching young children," the truth is very different. Just because the things they need to learn may appear simple from an adult's perspective, doesn't mean that the task of getting them to understand it, is easy! The process of learning will enable you to develop so many personal skills and attributes that can be transferred to many situations in life and in your future.

37. Sharing a Passion or Specialism through an After School Club

Many schools provide after school clubs and require teachers to run them. There will be plenty of scope for you to run a club that takes advantage of your interests or specialist skill sets. These clubs are great for the children and also great for the teachers, especially if you can share a passion and inspire other people to enjoy something you love. The clubs may not necessarily match up with the national curriculum, but that may well be the point; to give children an opportunity to experience something different that they wouldn't get the chance to in a normal school day.

The content of the clubs does depend on the school but surely if there is an educational benefit to the children and they are interested, then there is a need for the club. Perhaps it could be a hockey club, a gardening club, a street dance club or even a meditation and yoga club?

38. Nurturing the Self-Esteem of Children

This really is one of the true privileges of being a primary school teacher. Making sure children see themselves positively, so they can attempt the challenges of learning and life with confidence is a gift that you can give, that keeps on giving. Many children do not need such interventions but there may well be a few that you encounter in your professional life who need a bit more praise, encouragement and self-belief to feel good about themselves. Identifying this and subtly making a difference truly is one of the most rewarding aspects of being a primary school teacher.

39. Supporting Children with Special Education Needs

You may have children in your class who have special educational needs (SEN). There are many different kinds of circumstances that can affect a child's ability to learn or deal with school life in general. Examples of this could include dyslexia, Attention Deficit Hyperactivity Disorder (ADHD), Autistic Spectrum Disorder (ASD) or social, emotional and communication issues. Through no fault of their own, these children may find aspects of school life harder than other children. They may well need more of your time and expertise to help them to progress. Helping these children to enjoy school, to make progress in their learning and to feel positive about themselves and their education is a highly rewarding aspect of being a primary school teacher.

40. Strong Union Support

Unlike other industries or sectors of employment, there isn't one main union to support teachers in their professional lives in the U.K. You have a choice of union and they all offer services designed to provide help and guidance on professional matters.

You will pay a subscription fee once you are fully qualified and it can almost be thought of as professional insurance, as if in the worst case scenario, if something goes wrong or there is a problem, then your union will be there for you to help you sort the issue out. The three main teaching unions in England and Wales (in terms of their number of members) are the National Union of Teachers (NUT), the National Association of Schoolmasters Union of Women Teachers (NASWUT) and the Association of Teachers and Lecturers. The main union in Scotland is the Educational Institute of Scotland (EIS) and in Northern Ireland it is the Ulster Teachers' Union.

41. Special Days where Visitors come to School

This is one of the top 50 best things for many reasons. These days may not often come round very often but when they do, they break up the working week and can often provide quite a relaxing day, morning or afternoon where an individual or group of people take charge of your class and all you have to do is monitor behaviour and enjoy the show! You could experience visits from mobile theatre companies, animal sanctuaries, musicians, artists, drama workshops, authors, religious groups, scientists or even circuses! Any many others too, in fact you might be surprised at the variety of these visitors.

These days provide great learning and entertainment for the children and it's always a good idea to follow up this enthusiasm by expanding on the learning back in the classroom or feeding off the excitement to produce writing, posters or artwork.

42. Every Day is Different

Whilst every day will have certain similarities, for example teaching maths and English is likely to be a constant, there is still so much scope for variety. Even if you are teaching those two subject areas every day you won't be teaching the same thing in them - that really would be Groundhog Day! You never know how children in your class are going to react to each other and the lesson's objectives, so there is a degree of unpredictability even in the predictable aspects of daily life.

Combine this with the unpredictability of children in general and the variety of all the subjects in the national curriculum, and you can see how the picture is becoming clearer about the daily variety that you might experience. For some of you reading this, this will be at the top of the list of best things about being a primary school teacher because you will know that in many jobs every day is basically the same.

43. Time often appears to go Quickly Throughout the Working Day

Anyone who has ever had a job where they have painfully watched the clock edge towards 5 o'clock every day, or felt like they have done over an hour's worth of work only to look at the clock and see only 20 minutes has passed by, will be very pleased to hear that this rarely happens when working in a school.

The day is broken up nicely with registration, break times, assemblies, lunchtimes and the need to usually fit in 4 or 5 separate lessons into the day. This combined with the level of concentration required to actually teach all these lessons and run a class, mean that you don't really have time to twiddle your thumbs, be bored or watch the clock drag because before you know it, it is lunchtime and you are half way through the day!

44. Opportunities for Yearly Pay Increases

Whilst the salary progression structure has recently undergone an overhaul and isn't quite as simple as it used to be, there still remains the opportunity to increase your pay each year providing you do a great job, achieve or exceed the targeted or expected progress and show that you are meeting all the Teachers' Standards applicable to your next pay point. The idea of the new system is that it now enables head teachers and governors more freedom to reward teachers who are doing an amazing job. The fact that the opportunity still exists and that you can earn more every year puts this benefit in the top 50.

45. You can Dedicate Your Life to it if you so Wish

The job expands to the amount of time you are willing to dedicate to it. If you are the sort of person that likes to throw yourself and your life fully into your work or feel like you are lacking a sense of purpose in your life and want to dedicate yourself to something meaningful, then being a primary school teacher can definitely provide this for you.

If you don't feel that this applies to you then that is fine; you just need to make sure you manage your time effectively and focus on what is really important so that you can do a great job and always have time for other pursuits.

Whichever side of the fence you sit on, primary school teaching can provide you with the life that suits your needs.

46. Work with and Meet Many Other Professionals

You will not just spend your working life in isolation with just you and your class, you will get to interact with many other professionals who you can work with and learn from. You may get to meet educational psychologists, behaviour support workers, speech and language therapists, autistic spectrum disorder outreach workers, social services, specialist teachers, governors, occupational therapists, Special Educational Needs Co-ordinators (SENCOs), music therapists and dyslexia experts to name but a few. Combine this with all the other adults and support staff who work in a school and you can see how there is so much opportunity to expand your horizons, interact with other people and learn from other professionals. All of these aspects also contribute to the variety that the job offers.

47 Receiving Gifts and Kind Messages from Parents and Children

Of course no one goes into teaching to receive gifts from parents, but it makes the list because it is definitely one of the best things about the job. Perhaps at the end of term you may well receive gifts from parents or children, they may well indeed be generous and surprisingly thoughtful. But the best gift to receive is a letter from a parent saying what a good job you have done, how much they have noticed the difference in their child and their learning and how much their child loves coming to school with you as their teacher. Parents wouldn't write such a letter if they didn't mean it! And these kind messages of appreciation really make all your efforts worthwhile as you know in that moment that you have made a difference.

48. Taking part in Events like Comic Relief and Children in Need

Children love these events and schools across the land are famed for raising money and contributing to the overall success. These events are great as they teach children to put others first and to broaden their understanding of issues that are currently being faced around the wider world. And you might get to wear a silly costume!

The amount of participation depends on the school, some schools throw themselves head on into the events and others take a more relaxed approach, some may well not even join in at all. But the likelihood is that they will participate in some form and you will get to enjoy a different kind of day and possibly a great deal of fun too!

49. Decorating Your Class How You want it to Look

Personalising your class and making it look amazing easily makes the list as everyone loves to create a vibrant and fun learning environment.

Throughout your training you may have been squirrelling away ideas that you have stolen from other schools you have visited or developing your own ideas about how to best use the space. And then the day finally arrives where you get to make all the decisions and make your vision of what a classroom should be like come to life. The sense of pride and ownership is fantastic, and being able to stamp your individuality on a space that expresses who you are as a teacher easily makes this aspect of teaching in the top 50.

50. Freer Dress Code Restrictions than Many Jobs

The precise dress code in any school depends on the head teacher and senior management team, and their idea of what constitutes the right attire is for working with children. Some forward thinking and progressive heads allow a nicely relaxed dress code as they know that you are working with children at the end of the day, and if you are comfortable you can express yourself as a teacher. The heavily praised and successful education system in Finland, even permits teachers to not wear shoes in class and wear slippers along with loose fitting relaxing clothes. That said, you shouldn't turn up to your first encounter with a school dressed in your onesie, smart professional clothes is a safe option and then you can assess that particular school's attitude to the dress code.

A school may have a uniform for staff; for example, polo shirts with the school's logo on it or maybe they will expect nothing less than smart formal wear, some schools do still have quite traditional attitudes to certain things. Nevertheless, you may well be encouraged to wear sports gear when you teach P.E and indeed be pleasantly surprised at the range of acceptable clothes you can wear in your working day.

Now...There are actually 51 things on this list. We like to under-promise and over-deliver. We have saved possibly THE best thing about being a primary school teacher until last.

51. Guaranteed Joy and Fun Working with Children

This aspect of being a primary school teacher has to be up there amongst the top perks. There aren't many jobs that can provide potential joy and fun on a daily basis. Children love fun and laughter and are inherently funny themselves, the way they view the world and each other is still developing and their reactions to lessons and daily life is so unpredictable.

Having the ability as a teacher to laugh with the children whilst they learn will brighten up any day and go a long way to ensuring that the children in your class love to come to school, speak enthusiastically about their teacher and also serve to motivate them to learn more as they know that whatever you are going to teach them on any day will have an element of fun.

Sources of joy are plentiful too. Not just from the opportunity to help children and other adults but from the assortment of magically joyful moments that the job is guaranteed to provide.

Primary School Acronym Glossary

ADD - Attention Deficit Disorder

ADHD - Attention Deficit and hyperactivity disorder

AF - Assessment Focus

AFL - Assessment for Learning

APP - Assessing Pupils' Progress

ASD - Autistic Spectrum Disorder

AT - Attainment Target

ATL - Association of Teachers and Lecturers

BST - Behaviour Support Plan

CAF - Common Assessment Framework

CAMHS - Child and Adolescent Mental Health

CPD - Continuing Professional Development

CRB - Criminal Records Bureau

CVA - Contextual Value Added

DfE - Department for Education

EAL - English as an Additional Language

ECM - Every Child Matters

ELSA - Emotional Literacy Support Assistant

EP - Educational Psychologist

EWO - Educational Welfare Officer

EYFS - Early Years Foundation Stage

FFT - Fischer Family Trust

FSM - Free School Meals

G&T - Gifted and Talented

GTP - Graduate Training Program (now School Direct)

GTTR - Graduate Teacher Training Registry (now defunct)

HLTA - Higher Level Teacher's Assistant

HMI - Her Majesty's Inspectorate

HT - Head Teacher

ICT - Information and Communication Technologies

IEP - Individual education plan

INSET - In Service Education and Training

ITT - Initial Teacher Training

KS - Key Stage

KS1 - Key Stage 1

KS2 - Key Stage 2

LA - Local Authority

LA - Less Able/Lower Ability

LEA - Local Education Authority

LSA - Learning Support Assistant

MA - More Able

MFL - Modern Foreign Languages

NAHT - National Association of Head Teachers

NASWUT - National Association of Schoolmasters and Union Of Women Teachers

NC - National Curriculum

NQT - Newly Qualified Teacher

NUT - National Union of Teachers

OA - Off-site Activity

ODD - Oppositional Defiant Disorder

Ofsted - Office for Standards in Education

PE - Physical Education

PGCE - Postgraduate Certificate in Education

PM - Performance Management

PoS - Program of Study

PPA - Planning Preparation and Assessment

PRP - Performance Related Pay

PSHE - Personal Social Health Education

PTA - Parent Teacher Association

QCA - Qualifications and Curriculum Authority

QT - Qualified Teacher

QTS - Qualified Teacher Status

RAISEonline - Reporting and Analysis for Improvement through School Self-Evaluation

RE - Religious Education

SATs - Standard Assessment Tasks (or Tests)

SCITT - School Centred Initial Teacher Training

SDP - School Development Plan

SEAL - Social and Emotional Aspects of Learning

SEF - Self-Evaluation Form

SEN - Special Educational Needs

SENCO - Special Educational Needs Coordinator

SI - School Improvement

SIP - School Improvement Plan

SLA - Service Level Agreement

SMT - Senior Management Team

STA - Specialist Teaching Assistant

TA - Teaching Assistant

TDA - Training and Development Agency for schools

TES - Traveller Education Service

TES - Times Educational Supplement

TLR - Teaching and Learning Responsibility

UPN - Unique Pupil Number

URN - Unique Reference Number

VA - Voluntary Aided

VC - Voluntary Controlled

Useful Contacts and Links

The Future Teacher Foundation: Advice and innovative resources for aspiring, trainee, new and experienced teachers.

http://www.thefutureteacherfoundation.com

UCAS: The Portal to all Initial Teacher Education and Training

http://www.ucas.com/how-it-all-works/teacher-training

Teach First: The Charity that places graduates in schools for teacher training

http://www.teachfirst.org.uk

The Teaching Line: Advice on your application - 0800 389 2500

Troops to Teachers:

https://troopstoteachers.ctp.org.uk

Get into Teaching: The Government's Portal to ITET

http://www.education.gov.uk/get-into-teaching

The Student Loans Company: Loans to cover tuition fees

 http://www.slc.co.uk

GTP Wales: Primary site for Welsh graduate teacher training

http://teachertrainingcymru.org/node/62

Oversees Equivalence Information: The National Recognition Information Centre for the United Kingdom (UK NARIC)

UK NARIC, Oriel House, Oriel Road, Cheltenham, GL50 1XP.

Tel: 0870 990 4088; fax: 0870 990 1560.

Skills Test Helpline. Telephone: 0845 450 8867
Email: skillstests@pearson.com

GCSE Equivalence Testing: If you are lacking the required C grade in maths, science or English.

http://www.equivalencytesting.co.uk

BBC GCSE Bitesize: GCSE equivalence revision and learning resource.

http://www.bbc.co.uk/schools/gcsebitesize

Discover…

Over 150 complete Primary School lessons available from www.tes.co.uk

We were recently privileged to be asked to create premium resources for the Times Educational Supplement (TES) website – the largest network of teachers in the world. Our resources were selected out of over 800,000 resources and we were invited to create complete lessons for the launch of their new premium resources site.

We now have over 150 complete, ready-made lessons for EYFS, KS1 and KS2 age children, ready to download - which contain everything you need to easily teach an engaging and successful learning experience.

Most lessons contain PowerPoint presentation lesson introductions, starter activity, worksheets, differentiation, plenaries and clear teachers' notes plus creative and self/peer reflective opportunities. All lessons designed to meet the new curriculum which arrived in 2014.

Subjects covered: english, grammar, creative writing, fiction, non-fiction, guided reading, phonics, history, geography, science, art, PSHE, SEAL, cross-curricula learning and DT with new resources being added all the time.

168

Read More

Effective Primary School Teaching Made Easy: Do What Works From the Start by TFTF

This unique digital professional development package can be bought exclusively from the TES website and contains everything you need to know about mastering your trade and becoming an effective primary school teacher in the shortest time possible. Containing tips, shortcuts and simple yet detailed explanations on:

Data, differentiation, **assessment**, marking and feedback, **planning**, creating engaging learning experiences, **behaviour management**, how to effectively talk to children, **starters**, plenaries, **teaching inputs**, introductions, **designing learning activities**, questioning, **discussions**, learning objectives, **how to rapidly improve your teaching**, and so much more.

This package is the next step in your journey to becoming the outstanding teacher you deserve to be. Search for Effective Primary School Teaching Made Easy on **www.tes.co.uk** teaching resources.

About the Author

The Future Teacher Foundation was created by highly experienced education professionals who wanted to share their knowledge. TFTF exists to help new and aspiring teachers get their careers off to the best start possible and provide innovative teaching resources to assist all teachers in improving their professional lives.

We were recently privileged to be asked to create premium resources for the Times Educational Supplement (TES) website. We now have over 150 complete lessons and full units of work ready to download, which contain everything you need to teach an engaging learning experience. Lessons are also available from TeachersPayTeachers in the U.S.A.

If you have any questions or would just like to provide us with some feedback please contact us via email at support@thefutureteacherfoundation.com and we will reply to you as soon as possible.

Website: www.thefutureteacherfoundation.com

Facebook: The Future Teacher Foundation

Twitter: @The_FutureTeach

23537520R00099

Printed in Great Britain
by Amazon